MYTHS
IN MINUTES

NEIL PHILIP

MYTHS IN MINUTES

NEIL PHILIP

Quercus

CONTENTS

Introduction

Myths are sacred narratives. They tell of the creation of the world, of humankind and the animals, and of the doings of gods and heroes. More than that, each society's myths are a pattern book for all aspects of that society's culture. If we were imaginative enough, we could recreate any given culture from its mythology. In many cultures, myths have been orally transmitted, but even in literate societies, while the essence of myths tends to stay the same, the details and emphases may vary from one version to another, for myths are capable of containing a whole world of meanings.

Myths, like all stories, consist of words that feed into the imagination, and the imagination uses metaphor to give those words meaning. This transforming power of the imagination is the motive force of all mythology. The stories tend to unfold like dreams, from image to image, rather than rationally from event to event. These images encode deep truths about human nature and human behaviour. It is through transforming ideas into images that myths are able to retain their ambiguity, their flexibility and their many levels of interpretation. Mythology was not simply invented by the Greeks in order 'to cheer themselves up', as the French poet Guillaume Apollinaire put it. Myths are a fusion of people's creative, spiritual and social impulses. They have many functions – some religious, some aesthetic, some practical. They can be expressed in words, in images and symbols, in drama and dance, in ritual and ceremony. They are not just fanciful stories that people told in the past; they are the urgent organizing principles that shape societies and drive cultures.

The story of humankind is inseparable from the history of our attempts to answer the fundamental questions that haunt us about the great mysteries of life, death, being and becoming. From its origins in the vision quests of Ice Age shamans, through its role in transforming the human race from pastoral nomads to agrarian city-dwellers, right up to the rifts and fissures that threaten to tear the modern world apart along the faultlines of conflicting religious worldviews, myth matters. Myth is a vital element of our cultural inheritance. If we fail to understand it, we fail to understand ourselves.

What is mythology?

Mythology is fundamentally concerned with the great questions of life and death, of being and becoming. In the words of the artist Paul Gauguin, 'Where do we come from? What are we? Where are we going?' Nowadays we might consider such questions the territory of science, philosophy, or religion. But for most of human history, they have been the province of mythology. It is myth that has asked the questions, and myth that has provided answers.

Most people in the Western world have their first encounter with mythology through the myths of the ancient Greeks – stories that have become deeply entrenched within Western art and literature, both through Greek sources and through later Roman writers such as Ovid. But these classical myths are simply one example of the kinds of stories that have been told throughout the world since the dawn of time, in one long intellectual and spiritual quest that aims, essentially, to explain ourselves to ourselves.

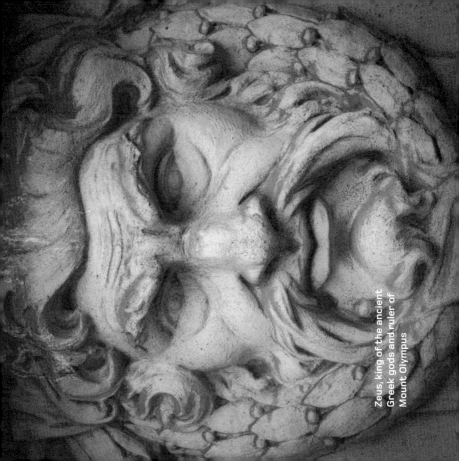

Zeus, king of the ancient Greek gods and ruler of Mount Olympus

A sense of the sacred

Long before the emergence of organized religion, humankind expressed an awareness of a spirit world existing alongside the visible world. It was into this spirit world that the earliest shamans ventured, in order to ensure success in the hunt.

A belief grew in the existence of gods and goddesses, inherent in the nature of things – powerful beings who controlled access to the beasts of land and sea, who granted or withheld the rain, who wielded the thunder and lightning or woke up the earth in spring. The earliest sacred spaces were naturally occurring ones – groves, springs, caves.

The worship of gods is ancient. At Laussel, in France, a sculpture representing a goddess of fertility and abundance holding a horn of plenty dates back to 25000 BCE. When the Greek city of Megara was founded, the first sacrifice was made to the gods of 'Before Building'; the Romans, who cannot be said to have lacked gods, still erected altars to 'the Unknown God'.

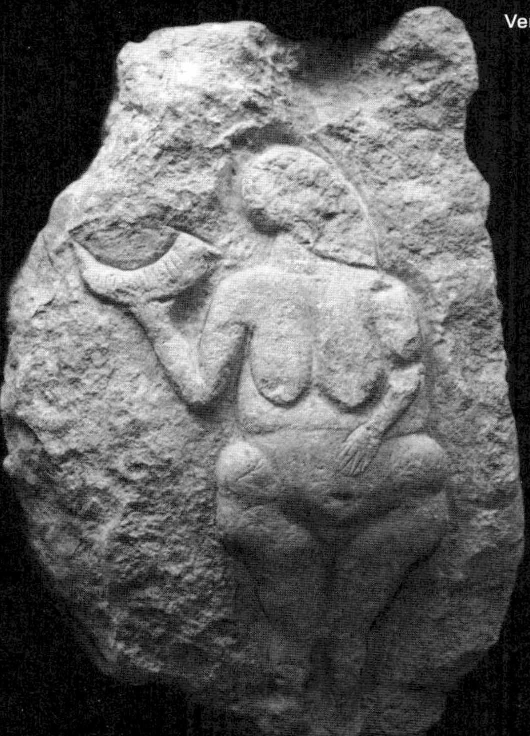

Venus of Laussel

Myth in shamanism

Palaeolithic visionaries made cave paintings during the Ice Age and have their equivalents in many cultures – Native-American medicine men, African witchdoctors, Aboriginal clever men and Siberian shamans, among others. Shamanism's 'techniques of ecstasy' use dance, drums and hallucinogenic drugs to induce a sense of out-of-body transcendence to penetrate and communicate with the spirit world.

San people believe the trickster Mantis created the world by dreaming; their shamans enter this same creative dream-state to exercise their powers of spirit travel, rainmaking and healing. In their trance state, Sami shamans first flew to a mountain at the centre of the world – the cosmic axis – before entering the spirit world, either above or below. The shaman might typically ride on a fish spirit, be guided by a bird spirit and protected by a reindeer spirit. A journey to the upper world of Saivo would be to plead for help of some kind; a journey to the underworld of Jabmeayimo would be to retrieve the soul of a sick person.

Sami shamanic drum

The earliest gods and goddesses

The names, natures and myths of the deities of prehistory are largely lost to us. Palaeolithic cave paintings dating back over 30,000 years reveal a world of shamanic vision quests remarkably similar to that of the San Bushmen of the Kalahari.

In the Stone Age, Neolithic and Chalcolithic peoples made stone and clay images of deities, often with animal and human features, and reflecting the new importance of agriculture. A 'sickle god' from around 5000 BCE is said to be an ancestor of the Greeks' Kronos. Most common of all is a great mother goddess with bird, snake and bee characteristics, mistress of the cosmic rain.

In the Bronze Age, after the migration into Europe of the patriarchal Indo-Europeans – inventors of the chariot and the wheel – a male sky god emerges, crossing the sky in the horse-drawn chariot of the sun. The myths of the Indo-Europeans overlaid those of Neolithic Europe and lie at the root of both European and Indian mythology.

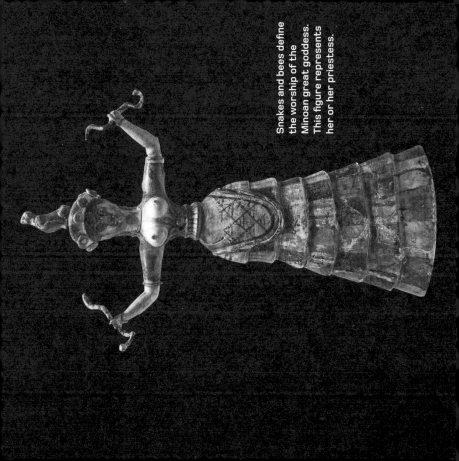

Snakes and bees define the worship of the Minoan great goddess. This figure represents her or her priestess.

Myth and the cosmos

Many cosmologies envisage the world as consisting of a number of layers, joined together by a central axis or world tree (such as the Norse Yggdrasill), above which the millstone of the celestial equator ground out the ages of the world. Before Copernicus, it was thought that the Earth was fixed and that the stars and planets revolved around it. In mythological terms this meant that the effects of the precession of the equinoxes were felt as a massive shifting of gears in the great machine of the heavens.

The name of the high god of the Incas, Viracocha, may be translated as 'the bearer of the mill', and the Incas pleaded with him, 'May the world not turn over'. The rise of the Roman cult of the god Mithras, usually shown slaying a bull, came from the need to find a new god capable of re-shaping the cosmos by 'slaying' the constellation of Taurus (the bull), and replacing it at the spring equinox with that of Aries. Mithras was worshipped and depicted as a 'kosmokrator', or cosmic ruler.

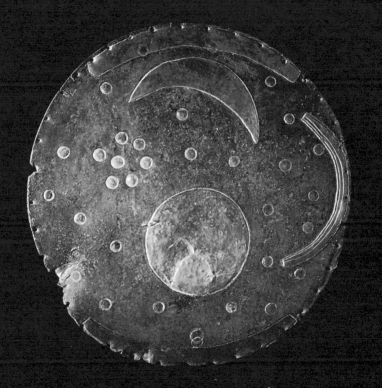

The Nebra sky disc shows the night sky around 1600 BCE, and the golden boat in which the sun traversed the sky.

Myth and time

It is by observing the dance of the stars in the night sky and the slow revolution of the planets that people measure time. Many ancient cosmologies were concerned with the instability of time, which they saw as being linked to the endless, yet cyclical, movement of the stars across the night sky.

The tension between the eternal and the temporal is central to myth. Mythic time is cyclical – rather than linear. Myths and rituals offer a way of entering the eternal present of this myth time and accessing its creative power. The longing to escape linear time, with its inevitable sense of an ending, is intrinsic to mythological thinking. In some mythologies, time is a kind of prison, from which we may eventually hope to escape. In Zoroastrian myth, Zurvan – 'Time' – is the androgynous pre-existing deity in the primal void, who gives birth to two sons, one born of his doubt, the other of his optimism. Zurvan could only curb the power of the evil son, Ahriman, by setting a limit to time itself, trapping Ahriman inside creation.

The Zoroastrian deity Zurvan

Myth and religion

I t is impossible to draw a firm line between mythology and religion, for both are concerned with humankind's relationship to the sacred. Religion is, in a sense, codified myth, yet the innate flexibility of myth is resistant to codification. So the more monolithic and dogmatic a religion becomes, the harder it is for it to accommodate a living mythology.

When the ancient Egyptian pharaoh Akhenaten declared the Aten – the disc of the sun – the sole god, the names of the other Egyptian gods were hacked from temple walls in an attempt to rub them out and destroy them in the netherworld. The result was chaos. 'The land was turned topsy-turvy, and the gods turned their backs on it. If anyone prayed to a god or goddess for help, they would not come. Their hearts were broken.' Shinto and Hinduism have rich mythologies because they are undogmatic. Religions that require the faithful to believe in the literal truth of a holy book, even if it contains mythological elements such as the Biblical story of the flood, are intrinsically antipathetic to myth.

Pharaoh Akhenaten worships the Aten, the disc of the sun.

Cultural context

In any attempt to understand mythology, cultural context is vital. Comparative mythology is fascinating (see pages 394–406), and it is reasonable, for example, to compare and contrast the many flood myths found around the world. However, it is a mistake to assume that, because one myth seems rather like another, the meanings of the two are the same. This is because myth is embedded in a particular culture, and carries meaning that expresses and validates that culture.

Myths are often not what they seem. There are myths of the Marind-Anim of West Papua that seem to be about sex, but are really about food. Conversely, myths of the Kwakwaka'wakw of Vancouver Island seem to be about food, but are really about sex. It is the context that creates the meaning. Even in the more familiar world of classical mythology, the supposed equivalence of the Greek and Roman gods is never exact. Roman Jupiter and Juno are as much Etruscan Tinia and Uni as they are Greek Zeus and Hera.

MASKED DANCERS—QÁGYUHL.

Masked Kwakwaka'wakw dancers

Myth and the environment

When the environmentalist James Lovelock developed his idea of the biosphere as a self-regulating entity, he asked the novelist William Golding to come up with a name for the hypothesis. Golding's choice was Gaia, the name of the ancient Greek goddess of the earth, the first creature to be born from the primeval chaos. Golding had recognized that Lovelock's theory was new only in its scientific dress, not in its essence.

In traditional societies, myth functions as a kind of mirror of the ecology and environment of a given culture. In the flat Orinoco delta, the Warao view the world from sea level, so for them the world is a narrow disc between the water and the sky. Peoples of the forest, or the desert, or the icy north, shape their mythologies in terms of their known worlds. The local mythology of the Ifugaos of the Philippines is so intimately tied in to their environment that their roll-call of over 1,500 separate gods – the seventy gods of reproduction, the five arthritis-afflicters and so on – are beings with no meaning to anyone but themselves.

A bronze bust of Gaia from the 1st century CE

Myth and society

The social function of myth is to bind a society together, to act as a charter for its laws and customs and to embed a culture within its environment. The cultural confidence of the Babylonians, for example, was built on an armature of mythology, which was expressed in the architecture of the city, in its customs and most fully in its elaborate New Year festival, the Akitu, in which the creation myth of the city's god, Marduk, was re-enacted over 12 days. Marduk represented the very essence of Babylon. So intimately were god and city entwined that the first act of any invading army was to carry off the cult statue of Marduk from his temple, thus plunging the city into mourning.

In tribal cultures, such as the Inuit of Canada or the Japanese Ainu, where the whole world is infused with a sense of mythic potentiality and every aspect of daily life is seen through the prism of mythology, there is no division between the world of myth and the world of reality. The two are intertwined and interdependent, and neither makes sense without the other.

Archaeological excavations at Ur, part of ancient Babylonia

Myths of ancient Egypt

The mythology of ancient Egypt can appear a sprawling muddle, with its countless overlapping gods, yet it remained remarkably stable over a period of some 3,000 years. Essentially, all the Egyptian gods were aspects of the creator Atum, 'the all', who manifested both as the sun god Ra and as Amun, the hidden god (the two being worshipped as Amun-Ra).

Individual gods had their own temple sanctuaries. That of Osiris, the ruler of the underworld, was at Abydos. Every year, in the last month of the inundation of the Nile on which the fertility of Egypt depended, the myths of Osiris were re-enacted there, telling the story of Osiris's murder, the grief of Isis and Nephthys (see pages 42–4) and the subsequent trial of Seth. After a grand battle between the supporters of Seth and Osiris, Osiris reappeared in triumph, and the djed-pillar, a stylized sheaf of corn symbolizing his rebirth, was erected. It was the resurrection of Osiris by mummification that gave Egyptians their hope of a new life after death in the Field of Reeds.

The great pyramids of Giza were the tombs of the pharaohs, before they established the Valley of the Kings, beneath a pyramid-shaped mountain sacred to the goddess Hathor.

The ancient Egyptian Creation

In ancient Egyptian mythology, before time began the creator, the Lord without Limit, rested in the form of a serpent with its tail in its mouth in the primal ocean Nun ("non-being"). He became aware of himself and manifested as Ra, the sun god. By an act of masturbation or auto-fellation, Ra created other gods, sneezing out Shu, the god of dry air, and spitting out Tefnut, the goddess of moist air. With his voice, using Heka (creative power), Sia (perception) and Hu (pronouncement), Ra called forth the elements of creation.

Heka, Sia and Hu accompanied Ra in his solar barque as he traversed the sky. He then created Ma'at, the goddess of truth and harmony, to watch over his creation. Causing the waters to recede, Ra stood on the Benben stone, the primal mound and model for the pyramids. Ra called forth from Nun all the plants, animals and birds; as he spoke their names, they came into being. The ancient Egyptians believed the annual inundation of the Nile was caused by the cosmic serpent coiled inside the cavern of Hapy, god of the flood, releasing the primal waters of Nun once more.

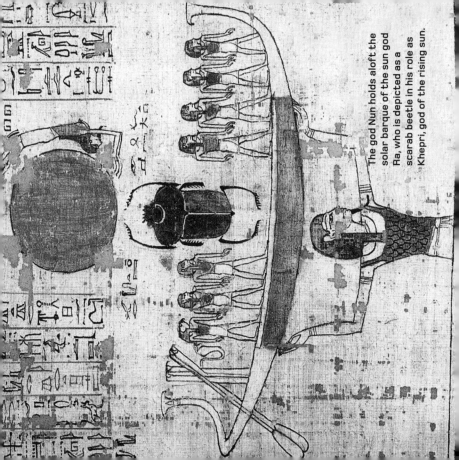

The god Nun holds aloft the solar barque of the sun god Ra, who is depicted as a scarab beetle in his role as Khepri, god of the rising sun.

The Eye of Ra

When the sun god Ra was creating the world, he sent his firstborn, Shu and Tefnut, out across the waters of the primal ocean of Nun. When they did not return, he sent his eye, the goddess Hathor, out to look for them. When she brought them back, she was angry, because another eye had grown on Ra's face, taking her place. She wept, and her bitter tears became the first human beings. Ra took Hathor and placed her on his brow, in the form of an enraged cobra. Now she would be with him as he ruled until, at the end of time, the world would once more be covered by the endless waters of Nun.

Hathor was a complex goddess, associated with sexual desire, fertility and love, but also with rage and destruction. When Ra sent her out as the savage lioness Sekhmet, she nearly destroyed humanity. Ra had to trick her by dying beer to resemble blood, which subdued her on drinking it. Egyptian pharaohs wore the cobra of Hathor on their brows, as a symbol of her 'devouring flame'. Hathor is also depicted as a cow.

Hathor (left) and Ra, depicted in the tomb of Queen Nefertari.

The earth and the sky

The sun god Ra's first children, Shu and Tefnut, gave birth to Geb, the dry earth, and Nut, the moist sky. Nut lay on top of Geb, and the sky mated with the earth, giving birth to the stars. Their jealous father Shu, the dry air, wrenched the two apart, holding the sky aloft with his hands and pinning down the earth with his feet.

Geb is usually depicted reclining on his side with one arm bent, his erect phallus pointing towards the sky. He was a god of fertility and vegetation; earthquakes were the 'laughter of Geb'. He was also known as the 'Great Cackler', thanks to the laugh he gave as he laid the egg from which the sun first emerged in the form of the Benu Bird, whose cry set time going.

Nut is depicted as a star-strewn body arched over the sky, her arms and legs outstretched to the cardinal points. She was thought to spread herself over the dead in the same way, and was often depicted on the underside of coffin lids.

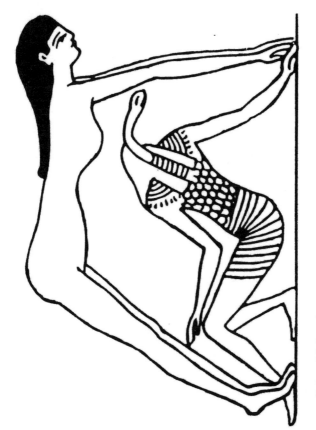

Nut and Geb, with a phallic snake—head

The Ennead

After the birth of the stars, the god Shu cursed his daughter, the sky goddess Nut, so that she could never give birth again in any of the twelve 30-day lunar months of the year. But Nut gambled with the moon god Thoth, the reckoner of time, and won five extra days from him, one to be added to each of five lunar months. On these days Nut gave birth to five children: Osiris, Blind Horus, Seth, Isis and Nephthys. These joined Shu, Tefnut, Geb and Nut to form the Ennead, the nine greatest gods of Egypt, with Ra at their head.

Osiris was the model of an earthly king, before becoming the ruler of the underworld; Seth, who lived in the desert wilderness, was the embodiment of disorder. Each of them married one of their sisters, Osiris taking Isis and Seth, Nephthys. Blind Horus, or the Elder Horus, a falcon god of the sky, was worshipped at Letopolis. Blind Horus was slain by his brother Seth. He was then reborn as Horus, the son of Isis and Osiris, to continue the struggle between himself and Seth.

Osiris, flanked by Isis and Nephthys

Ra's night journey

'**H**ail to you, Ra, perfect each day!' opens one of the hymns to the sun god, the uncreated creator who 'traverses eternity, and to whom each day is but a moment.'

The sun god took three main forms: Khepri, the scarab beetle, who was the rising sun; Ra, the sun's disc, who was the midday sun; and Atum, an old man leaning on a stick, who was the setting sun. Each evening, as the sun reached the west, the sky goddess Nut swallowed it. Each morning, she gave birth to it once more in the east. Ra's nightly journey was not without peril. As he sailed through the netherworld in his night barque, demons assailed him, led by the monstrous serpent Apophis. In the darkest hour before dawn, Apophis would make his most desperate attack. Each night, the chaos god Seth would spear the serpent and Ra, in the form of a cat, would cut off its head. And so chaos was held at bay. The next night, Apophis would be lying in wait once more. If Apophis were ever to vanquish Ra, the sun would fail to rise.

The night barque of Ra

Ra's secret name

Egyptian texts speak of 'tens of thousands and thousands of gods' – so many that they could not be numbered. Even Ra, who created himself and who made the heavens and the earth, had so many names that the other gods did not know them all.

Isis, mistress of magic, wanted to learn the names of all things, so that she should become as great as Ra. At last, the only name she did not know was Ra's own secret name. As Ra sailed across the sky each day, he grew old. His mouth grew slack and his spittle dribbled to the ground. Isis gathered the spittle and shaped it with earth to create a snake, which she left in Ra's path. The snake bit Ra, who fell with a terrible cry, poisoned. Isis said she would save him if he told her his secret name. Dying, Ra allowed his mind to be searched by Isis, and for the name that he had kept secret since the dawn of time to flow from his heart into hers. By the power of Ra's name, Isis commanded the poison to flow out of his body and spill to the ground. Ra was made strong again and Isis's knowledge was complete.

The goddess Isis

The murder of Osiris

The god Osiris once ruled as king on Earth. He taught the ancient Egyptians how to live, how to farm and how to make and use tools. His sister-wife, Isis, taught the women how to make bread and beer, how to spin and weave and how to care for children and the elderly.

Osiris set out around the world, to teach all humankind about his discoveries. For this he was called Wennefer, 'the eternally good'. Seth, his brother, was jealous. When Osiris made Isis, and not Seth, his regent, Seth vowed to kill him, to take his throne and marry Isis himself. He invited Osiris to a banquet, where he revealed a marvellous cedarwood chest and promised to give it to whoever fitted inside it. Everyone tried, but no one fitted until, at last, Osiris climbed in. Seth slammed the lid down, nailed it shut and threw the chest into the Nile. Isis found the dead king, but when she left his body unattended, Seth cut it into fourteen pieces. Scattering the pieces across Egypt, Seth said, 'It is not possible to destroy the body of a god, but I have done so.'

Isis stands behind Osiris, who wears the Atef crown and carries his crook and flail.

Isis and Osiris

Osiris was killed and dismembered by his evil brother, Seth. His sister-wife, Isis, and her sister, Nephthys, gathered up his scattered body parts. Whenever they found a piece, Isis used her magic to make a wax model of it. She left each wax model in the care of a priest at a shrine to Osiris, thus establishing his worship across the whole of ancient Egypt.

Seeing the sisters gather the god's dismembered body, the sun god Ra took pity on them. He sent the jackal god Anubis and the ibis god Thoth to help them. Anubis embalmed Osiris's body with unguents. Once the body was pieced back to its true shape, Anubis wrapped it in bandages, so making the first mummy. Isis changed herself into a kite and, hovering over the mummified Osiris, fanned the breath of life back into him for long enough to conceive a child, Horus, who would later avenge his father. Then Osiris, who is always depicted as a mummy, took his place as lord of the underworld, where he was told he must live for millions of years, until the end of the world.

Isis mourns Osiris

The rivalry of Horus and Seth

The god, Blind Horus, was slain by his brother Seth, then reborn to Isis and Osiris. The new Horus continued the struggle with Seth, contending with him for 80 years, before Ra awarded him the kingship of Egypt. At one point Seth tore out Horus's left eye, while Horus cut off Seth's testicles. On another occasion, they challenged each other to a race in stone boats. Horus won by making his boat of cedarwood, but coating it with gypsum to resemble stone. His boat floated, while Seth's, made from a mountain peak, sank.

In the end, both gods retrieved their body parts. Horus's eye was healed by the goddess Hathor, and this restored *wedjat* (eye) became the most common ancient Egyptian amulet, a symbol of wholeness, protection, strength and perfection. As god of the dawn, Horus was worshipped as Horemakhet (Horus in the horizon); as a sun god he was blended with Ra as Ra-Horakhty; in other forms he was worshipped as Horus the son of Isis, Horus the avenger of his father and as Horus the child.

Seth and Horus adoring Pharaoh Ramesses II, in the Small Temple at Abu Simbel.

Mummification

The story of the death and resurrection of the god Osiris was the foundation myth that offered ancient Egyptians the hope of new life after death. At first, this was only for the king, who 'became' Osiris in the underworld but, in the end, the promise of rebirth into eternal life was open to all Egyptians.

All rituals of death, of mummification, entombment and ritual remembrance were aimed at ensuring new life after death in the Field of Reeds, a perfected version of ancient Egypt. Care had to be taken of all the elements that made up a complete person: the physical body, the name, the shadow, the *ka* (individuality), the *ba* (spiritual essence) and the *akh* (a combination of everything else, the form of the blessed dead). The body had to be preserved by mummification in rituals that identified the deceased with the god Osiris. Spells from the Pyramid Texts, the Coffin Texts and the Book of the Dead enabled them to speak, breathe, eat and drink in the netherworld. One crucial spell was 'for not dying again in the realm of the dead.'

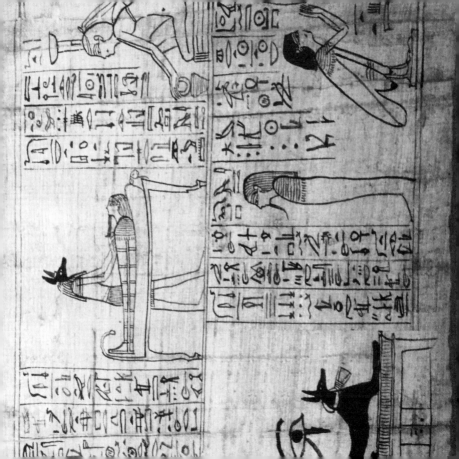

The afterlife

Egyptians wanted to live as perfected beings in the Field of Reeds. This was the domain of Osiris, the lord of the dead. In it, the blessed dead gathered in rich crops of barley and emmer wheat – the abundant harvests that are joyously depicted on the walls of their tombs.

First, the newly dead must be judged in the Hall of the Two Truths, which was reached via a path beset with terrible dangers. There, the heart of the deceased was weighed in a balance against the feather of *maat* (harmony). The god Anubis checked the balance, and the scribe god Thoth recorded the results on leaves from the tree of life. If the heart, heavy with evil thoughts and acts, outweighed the feather, it would be gobbled up by the she-monster Ammut. To escape this dreadful fate, Egyptians made a Negative Confession, listing all the sins they had not committed. Those who passed the test were then led by Horus into the presence of Osiris and the judges of the underworld, who judged each case on its merits.

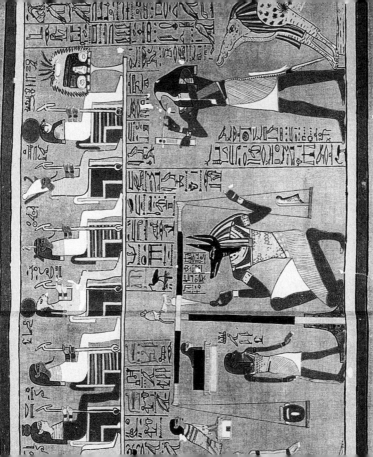

The Papyrus of Ani depicts the weighing of Ani's heart before he can enter the Field of Reeds.

Myths of Mesopotamia

In the fourth millenium BCE, Mesopotamia was the cradle of Western civilization. Successive Mesopotamian cultures – the Sumerians, Akkadians, Babylonians, Assyrians and Persians – shared very similar mythologies. The epic of the semi-divine hero Gilgamesh, for example, the first account of the flood myth later found in the Christian Bible, and the story of Gilgamesh's vain search for immortality, existed in the Sumerian, Akkadian and Babylonian languages.

Mesopotamian myth sought a balance between the twin threats of flood and drought, and centred on the promise of the paradise garden of Dilmun against the threat of the parched desert of the underworld. Creation myths of a primal flood reflect the constant process of draining and irrigation required to create fertile land. The city was at the heart of Mesopotamian culture, and each city had its own god. The god of Babylon was Marduk. When Babylon was conquered by the Assyrians in 691 BCE, the myths of Marduk were reattributed wholesale to the Assyrian god, Ashur.

The Ishtar gate from Babylon

The Babylonian Creation

The Babylonians recited and enacted their creation story each New Year, at the spring equinox. The intention was to re-establish the ordered universe described in the story and to keep the forces of chaos at bay 'until time is old'.

At the beginning of all things were two seas – male Apsu, the sweet water, and female Tiamat, the salt water. A third deity, Mummu (mist), accompanied them. Apsu and Tiamat gave birth to the silt that formed where rivers met the sea, and to the horizons of sky and earth. The horizons, Anshar and Kishar, gave birth to Anu, the sky, and Anu made Ea, the god of earth, water and magic. The clamour of these new gods disturbed Apsu and Tiamat while resting. They took counsel with Mummu; Tiamat pleaded for indulgence, but Apsu and Mummu were determined to destroy the younger gods. On hearing this, wise Ea cast a spell that sent Apsu into a deep sleep. Ea claimed kingship of the gods, killed Apsu and imprisoned Mummu. Ea then created a sacred chamber in which to rest, and named it Apsu.

The first cuneiform tablet of the Babylonian creation myth, the Enuma Elish

The battle of Marduk and Tiamat

The Babylonian Marduk (sun-child) was born to Ea and Damkina in the deep peace of the sacred chamber of Apsu. Tiamat, the mother of all, was encouraged by her children to fight this powerful new god. She gave birth to monsters, such as the scorpion-man and the centaur. She made the firstborn, Kingu, leader of her troops, and invested him with the Tablet of Destinies. Tiamat herself turned into a ferocious dragon.

Marduk agreed to fight Tiamat if the other gods agreed to accept him as their king in victory, which they did. In combat, Marduk overcame Tiamat in her dragon form, slicing her in two; from the two halves, he created the sky and the earth. The rivers Tigris and Euphrates sprang from her eyes. Marduk killed Kingu and took the Tablet of Destinies for himself. He used them to create the cosmos, establishing the calendar and ordering the planets and stars. From Kingu's blood, Marduk created mankind, to serve the gods. Finally, he founded the city of Babylon to house his great temple, the House of the Foundation of Heaven and Earth.

Primeval battles between chaos monsters and sun gods like the ones shown in this later Assyrian relief are a repeated theme in Mesopotamian mythology.

Inanna, queen of heaven

The Sumerian goddess of love, Inanna, known to the Babylonians as Ishtar, was the queen of heaven and earth. She was the daughter of Enki (Babylonian Ea), the god of wisdom. One myth tells how Inanna won from Enki the sacred *me*, the powers he used to establish order in the world.

Innan visited her father and, on entering his shrine, Enki welcomed her with cold water to refresh her heart, and beer, which they drank together at the Table of Heaven. Once drunk, Enki offered Inanna the *me*, one by one: the throne of kinship, the art of lovemaking and the ability to descend into the underworld. With each one, Inanna replied, 'I take them!' She put the *me* into the Boat of Heaven and sailed across the sky to her city of Uruk. When Enki sobered up, he summoned his servant Isimud and asked for the *me*. Isimud told him he had given them to Inanna. Enki sent demons to reclaim the *me*, but Inanna's servant Ninshubur repelled them. Inanna placed the *me* in her temple; power had transferred for all time from father to daughter.

Inanna resting her foot on a lion

Inanna's descent into the underworld

Inanna had to choose between a farmer and a shepherd for her husband. She chose the shepherd, Dumuzi, and gave him the kingship of her city, Uruk. While he was away, Inanna used her powers to descend into the parched underworld.

At each of seven doors, Inanna was stripped of her clothing, her jewels and her signs of authority. She arrived naked and defenceless before the throne of her sister Ereshkigal, who sentenced her to death and had her body hung up on a spike. Inanna's servant Ninshubur begged the gods to help, but they refused. Enki, Inanna's father, made two creatures from the dirt beneath his fingernails; they took her food and water, to bring her back to life. Once Inanna was revived, the judges of hell refused to let her return to life unless someone else took her place. She told them to take her husband. Demons pursued Dumuzi and dragged him into the underworld. Thereafter, he spent six months of every year in that barren land. When he emerged each spring, bringing fertility, his sister Geshtinanna took his place.

Dumuzi is tortured by demons in the underworld.

Nergal and Ereshkigal

The destructive god Nergal was the son of Enlil, the high god of the Babylonian pantheon, and his wife, Ninlil. When the gods were planning a banquet, the sky god Anu sent his servant Kakka down into the underworld to tell its queen Ereshkigal that, since it was impossible for her to come, she should send her servant to fetch her portion. So she sent her servant Namtar up the long stairway to heaven.

When he arrived, all the feasting gods rose and bowed, except for rude Nergal. Ereshkigal heard of this disrespect and demanded that the god be sent to her for punishment. The wise god Ea armed Nergal with fourteen demons and, when Nergal was admitted to the presence of Ereshkigal, he attacked her with those demons. He grabbed Ereshkigal by the hair and pulled her from her throne, intending to cut off her head. She told him he could be her husband, with kingship over the earth and the tablet of wisdom in his hand. So he kissed her; the underworld now had both a king and a queen.

Erishkigal, Queen of the Night

The story of the flood

Utnapishtim lived in the city of Shuruppak, on the banks of the river Euphrates. The city teemed with people, and their busy clamour disturbed the peace. In a council of the gods, Enlil, Babylonian god of the air, proposed the destruction of the human race, and resolved to let loose a mighty flood. Enki, the god of wisdom, whispered words of warning to Utnapishtim, telling him to tear down his house of reeds and construct a boat instead.

Utnapishtim built the boat and loaded it with his possessions, his family and the beasts, both wild and tame. That evening, the gods unleashed the storm. Adad, lord of the storm, rode at its head, and the gods of the abyss unleashed the waters from below. Even the gods cowered from the tempest and wept at the destruction. On the seventh day, the storm calmed and Utnapishtim's boat landed on a mountaintop. He sent out a dove, a swallow and a raven to search for land. He made a sacrifice to the gods, and they accepted his offering. Enlil, repenting, made Utnapishtim and his wife immortal, to live forever at the mouth of the river.

The earliest account of the flood, on a tablet from the Library of Nineveh, 7th century BCE.

Gilgamesh and Enkidu

In Babylonian mythology, Gilgamesh, the king of Uruk, was two-thirds god, but one-third man, and so he was doomed to die. He was a cruel ruler and the people of Uruk prayed to be freed from his tyranny. Aruru, goddess of creation, made a wild man named Enkidu out of clay and sent him to kill Gilgamesh. In response, the king sent one of the sacred prostitutes from the temple of Ishtar to seduce and tame Enkidu. When she brought him back to Uruk, he and Gilgamesh wrestled, but neither could defeat the other. They became friends; now there were two tyrants.

The gods sent a monster, Humbaba, to defeat them, but Gilgamesh and Enkidu overcame him, with the help of the sun god Shamash. When Gilgamesh rejected the goddess Ishtar, she begged Anu to send down the Bull of Heaven to destroy him, but Gilgamesh and Enkidu killed that too. So Ishtar killed Enkidu with a fever, and sent him to join the bird-winged spirits in the House of Dust. Gilgamesh was devastated at the loss of his friend, and set out to discover the secret of immortality.

Gilgamesh, holding a lion cub.

Gilgamesh and the plant of eternal life

The death of Enkidu cast Gilgamesh into grief. He foresaw his own death, and was afraid. So he set off in search of the only human ever to have been granted immortality – Utnapishtim, sole survivor of the great flood, rescued by the gods and set to live in the paradise garden of Dilmun.

When he arrived at Mashu, the great mountain that guards the rising and setting sun, Gilgamesh found two Scorpions (half-man and half-dragon) guarding the gates. They allowed him to travel through the darkness of the mountain into the garden of the gods. There he met the sun god, Shamash, who told him he would never achieve the eternal life he sought. By the seashore at the edge of the world, Gilgamesh found Siduri, goddess of brewing, who told him how to reach Utnapishtim's ferryman. Utnapishtim revealed to Gilgamesh the existence of a plant that would make an old man young. Gilgamesh took the plant, but a snake stole and ate it. The Babylonians said that was why snakes can shed their skins and rejuvenate, but men grow old and die.

This cylinder-seal, dating to c.2300 BCE, depicts the sun god Shamash (centre) with rays rising from his shoulders.

The disappearance
of Telepinu

O ne day, without warning, the Hittite god of farming and fertility Telepinu flew into a rage. Beside himself with anger, he put his left shoe on his right foot and his right shoe on his left foot, before leaving for the barren steppe. With Telepinu gone, mist covered the land; logs would not burn in the fireplace; sheep neglected their lambs, and cows their calves; springs dried up and no grain grew. The sun god Shamash held a feast for a thousand gods, but they could not satisfy their hunger or their thirst.

The storm god Adad grew anxious about Telepinu, his son, and sent an eagle out to search every mountain and valley for him, but with no luck. The mother goddess Hannahanna sent her sacred bee to find Telepinu, to sting his hands and feet and bring him back to the gods. But when Telepinu returned, he was as angry as ever. Kamrusepa, goddess of healing, purified him with an eagle's wing. The doorkeepers of the underworld opened the seven doors, and the black rage of Telepinu disappeared into the dark. Telepinu was himself again and fertility was restored.

The weather-god, Adad, father of Telepinu

Baal's death and resurrection

The Ugarit god of fertility, thunder and lightning, Baal was the son of the high god El and his wife Ashtoreth. Baal had the craftsman god Kothar design him a wonderful palace, but without any windows, so that his brother Yamm could not spy on his concubines. Kothar left just one window, so that Baal could still send down his rain and lightning.

Baal's sister Anath, goddess of love and war, invited Baal's enemies to a feast, and slaughtered them all, hanging their heads around her neck. One enemy was not among them – Mot, the god of death. Baal swore he would not pay tribute to him, but Mot's reply was so terrifying that Baal declared himself Mot's eternal slave. Soon Baal died. Drought and famine wracked the land for seven years in the deadly grip of Mot. Anath searched for Baal, and when Mot boasted he had chewed Baal up, she cut Mot into pieces, burned him, minced him and sowed him in the ground. Both Baal and Mot came back to life, and the sun goddess Shapash persuaded them to have separate kingdoms, above and below.

Baal wielding
a thunderbolt

Myths of ancient Greece

The notion of a consistent pan-Hellenic body of mythology and pantheon of gods, as laid out by mythographers such as Apollodorus, is misleading: ancient Greek myth was intensely local, rooted in kinship group, countryside and city. For the ancient Greeks, myth started at home, with the protective and ancestral gods of the household. These included the Agathos Daimon (Good Spirit), the tutelary spirit of the place, represented as a snake, and the fire of the goddess Hestia, which burned perpetually at the hearth. There were gods of the locality – the rural god Melampus worshipped at Aegosthena, for example. And there were guardian gods of the polis, or city-state. The guardian deity of the city of Mantineia was Poseidon Hippios (Poseidon the horseman). His image was on the city's coinage; his sanctuary – forbidden on pain of death to all but his priest – was at the city gates. As the god of both underground water and of horses, Poseidon – conventionally thought of as the god of the sea – was a good choice of patron for a horse-breeding people living in an inland city with problematic drainage.

The Trojan priest
Laocoön and his sons
attacked by serpents

The ancient Greek Creation

The ancient Greeks told several stories about how the world came into being. Hesiod's Theogony (eighth century BCE) recounts an initial state of Chaos, envisaged as a chasm or gap from which Gaia, the earth, was born, followed by Tartarus, the underworld, and Eros, the god of love and desire.

Next came Darkness and Night, who mated and gave birth to Brightness and Day. Other children of Night included Death, Sleep, the Moirai or Fates and that essential element of life, Eris or Strife. The earth Gaia then brought Ouranos (the sky), the Ourea (the mountains) and Pontos (the sea) into being. Gaia mated with Ouranos to produce a number of children, including the Titans, the Cyclopes and the Hundred-Handers, all of whom were imprisoned in the earth – that is, in the body of Gaia, their mother – by jealous Ouranos.

Some myths speak of a primal egg, laid by either Gaia or the goddess Eurynome, from which the cosmos was born.

The god of desire, Eros was one of the primordial Greek gods. Later texts demote him to the naughty child of Aphrodite, goddess of love.

The gods of Olympus

O nce they had defeated the Titans (see page 80), the Olympian gods drew lots to split up the world between them. Zeus became ruler of the sky, Poseidon of the sea and Hades of the underworld. Zeus was the supreme god, and ruled over all others from Mount Olympus.

Besides Zeus and Hades (rarely seen as a god because he inhabits the underworld), there were twelve main Olympian gods. Four of them were children of Kronos and Rhea: Hestia, goddess of the hearth; Demeter, the corn goddess; Hera, goddess of marriage and wife of Zeus; and Poseidon. Authorities differ over the remaining eight, but most name Aphrodite, goddess of love; Artemis, goddess of hunting; Apollo, god of the sun and of the arts; Ares, god of war; Hephaestos, god of fire and metalworking; Athena, goddess of war and wisdom; Dionysos, god of wine and ecstasy; and Hermes, the messenger of the gods. The life of the gods on Mount Olympus is said to have been perfect bliss, and yet is depicted in myths as being full of strife, discord and betrayal.

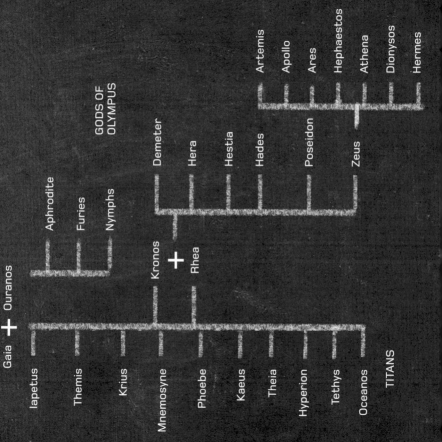

The Titans

When jealous Ouranos imprisoned the twelve Titans – six male and six female – in the body of their mother, Gaia, angry Gaia created a sickle of adamant, which she gave to the youngest of the children, Kronos. The next time Ouranos lay with Gaia, Kronos reached out and castrated him with the sickle. Kronos threw the severed genitals of Ouranos into the ocean, where they floated to Cyprus.

The Titans were freed and, under the leadership of Kronos, now ruled the world. Kronos married his sister Rhea, who gave birth to the first of the Olympian gods: Hestia, Demeter, Hera, Hades and Poseidon. Gaia had told Kronos that he, like Ouranos, was destined to be overthrown by his own child, so he swallowed each baby as it was born. Gaia stole away a sixth baby, Zeus, to be raised in secret in Crete. When he was grown, Zeus tricked Kronos into vomiting up the gods. Zeus then freed the Cyclopes, who gave him a thunderbolt that helped him gain victory in the war between the Titans and the Olympians.

The Titan goddess Gaia (reclining), and the god Kronos (standing).

The origins of the human race

The gods made several attempts to create human beings. Their first, the Golden Race, was peaceful and wise but produced no children, so died out naturally. The people of the Silver Race were mean-spirited and foolish; Zeus destroyed them, because they failed to honour the gods. The Titan Prometheus is said to have fashioned a third, Bronze Race, from clay; Athena, goddess of wisdom, breathed life into them. When these people sacrificed a bull to Zeus, Prometheus hid the meat beneath the bull's hide. He covered the bones in tempting fat and asked Zeus to choose which portion should be for the gods. Zeus chose the bones and was so angry, he withheld the gift of fire from humans. Prometheus stole fire from the chariot of the sun and gave it to humanity. He gave humans other gifts, such as the ability to think. The Bronze Race disappointed Zeus, so he sent a flood to wipe it out. The only survivors were Deukalion, son of Prometheus, Pyrrha, daughter of Prometheus's brother Epimetheus, and Pandora (the first mortal woman, sent by Zeus with a forbidden jar, which she opened to release all the ills of the world).

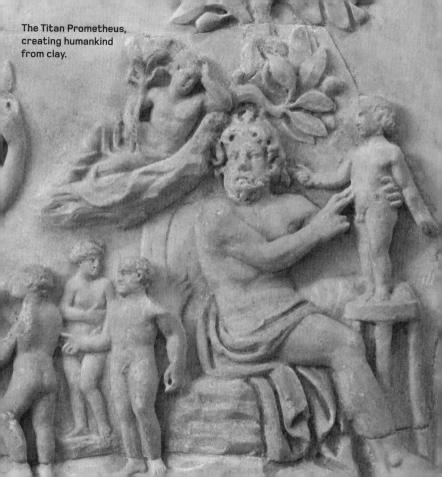

The Titan Prometheus, creating humankind from clay.

The punishment of Prometheus

Prometheus and his brother Epimetheus were Titans who had battled against their own kind alongside the gods of Olympus. When Prometheus stole fire to give to mankind, he enraged Zeus, who turned Epimetheus into a monkey and sentenced Prometheus to 30,000 years of punishment.

Chained to a rock in the Caucasian Mountains, Prometheus was visited every night by a great eagle that pecked out his liver; each day, Zeus renewed the liver, so that the torture was never-ending. One day Prometheus warned Zeus against his pursuit of a sea nymph called Thetis, saying that any son borne to her would be greater than his father. Zeus gave up on Thetis, and allowed Herakles (his son by Alkmene) to free Prometheus, by shooting the eagle dead on his way to win the Golden Apples of the Hesperides. In return, Prometheus told Herakles how to win the apples, by temporarily taking the place of Atlas, a Titan who bore the world on his shoulders, while Atlas himself fetched the apples. Prometheus later joined the immortals on Mount Olympus.

Prometheus chained to the crag, the subject of Aeschylus' play *Prometheus Bound*.

Zeus and Hera

Zeus, ruler of the sky and of the gods, reigned supreme over Olympus, enforcing his authority with his thunderbolts and the strength of his bare hands. Poseidon, Athena and Zeus's wife, Hera, challenged his power on one occasion, conspiring to bind him, but he was freed by Thetis, the sea nymph, who was also the mother of Achilles. Some sources claim that Zeus punished Hera for her actions, suspending her from a golden chain, with anvils hanging from her feet.

Hera was the goddess of marriage, yet her relationship with Zeus was stormy, largely because of his infidelity. In her jealousy, Hera sought revenge on many of Zeus's lovers. When the Titan Leto was pregnant by Zeus with Aphrodite and Apollo, Hera denied her any place to give birth. When Leto at last found the floating island of Delos, Hera kept Eileithyia, the goddess of childbirth, away from her. Zeus and Hera produced three children: Ares, god of war; Eileithyia, goddess of childbirth; and Hebe, goddess of youth. A fourth child, the smith god Hephaestos, is said to be Hera's alone.

Zeus and Danae

Kings of Argos were descendants of Epaphos, the son of Zeus and Io. Twin male heirs to the throne, Akrisios and Proitos, quarrelled in the womb and grew up fighting each other. They divided the kingdom in two, with Akrisios ruling in Argos and Proitos in Tiryns.

Akrisios had a daughter, Danae. When he consulted the Delphic oracle as to whether he would have a son, the oracle foretold that Danae would bear a son, who would kill him. The fearful king built a chamber of bronze below his courtyard, with just a chink in the roof to let in light and air. Here he imprisoned Danae and her nurse. Zeus seduced Danae by turning himself into a shower of gold that spilled into her lap. She gave birth to a boy, the hero Perseus (see pages 120–2). She and the nurse raised him in secret until, when he was three or four years old, Akrisios heard his playful cries. The king executed the nurse and locked Danae and Perseus in a chest that was thrown into the sea. He expected them to die, but they were rescued in a fisherman's net.

Zeus impregnates Danae in a shower of gold.

Leda and the swan

Leda was the wife of Tyndareos, king of Sparta. Zeus seduced her, taking the form of a swan. Tyndareos lay with his wife the same night, and Leda gave birth to four children: Helen and Polydeuces, who were fathered by Zeus; and Castor and Clytemnestra, who were fathered by Tyndareos.

Each of these children was to play a significant role. Helen was a great beauty, abducted by Theseus to be his bride, but rescued by Polydeuces and Castor. All the leading Greeks vied for Helen's hand. Tyndareos gave her to Menelaos, but she left him for Paris, thus sparking the ten-year Trojan War. Clytemnestra married Agamemnon, king of Mycenae. She never forgave him for sacrificing their daughter Iphigeneia to secure fair winds to Troy; on his return she killed him. Their son, Orestes, later took revenge for her act. Polydeuces and Castor were called the Dioscuri. When Castor was dying, Polydeuces begged Zeus to allow him to die too; instead, Castor was allowed to share in his brother's immortality, and the pair spent alternate days in Hades and on Mount Olympus.

Aphrodite and Ares

Aphrodite, the goddess of love, was born from the sea foam that gathered around the severed genitals of Ouranos (see page 80). Only the virgin goddesses Athena, Artemis and Hestia were safe from the pains and pleasures she provoked.

Aphrodite was married to the lame artificer god, Hephaestos, but their marriage was not a happy one. Aphrodite took the war god Ares as her lover, and the sun god Helios saw them making love. He told Hephaestos, who used his skill as a smith to fashion an invisible, unbreakable net to hang over his bed; when the lovers lay down, the net descended, trapping them in the act. Hephaestos then invited all the gods and goddesses to come and view the humiliated pair. The goddesses stayed away, but Poseidon, Hermes and Apollo did not hesitate to come. They laughed at the unhappy pair, and Apollo and Hermes agreed it would be worth being caught in such a trap in order to sleep with Aphrodite. Eventually, Poseidon persuaded Hephaestos to free the lovers on condition that Ares paid a fine.

Aphrodite and Adonis

The handsome youth Adonis is an import into Greek mythology from western Asia; his story has many parallels with the Babylonian's Dumuzi (see page 60). Adonis is said to be the product of incest between Myrrha and her father Theias, king of the Assyrians. Myrrha crept into Theias's bed in the dark, and when he eventually lit a lamp to see his mysterious lover, he tried to kill her. Myrrha fled and was later turned into a myrrh tree. A boar gored the tree and Adonis was born.

Aphrodite and Persephone both fell in love with Adonis and took their dispute to Zeus, who gave Adonis to each of them for one-third of the year, leaving Adonis free to choose for the remaining third (in some versions of the story, Zeus allots six months each). Adonis chose Aphrodite. Ovid tells how the pair often went hunting, and how Adonis was killed by a wild boar, the first anemones springing from his blood. Adonis is, in essence, a god of fertility and vegetation. He is on earth in the growing season, and in the underworld during fallow periods.

Apollo and the python

Apollo was the god of prophecy, archery, music and the arts; as Phoebus Apollo, he was god of the sun. The son of Zeus and the Titaness Leto, Apollo was fully grown in a matter of days, having been fed on ambrosia by the goddess Themis. Themis could foresee the future, and Apollo, schooled in divination by the god Pan, became the god of prophecy. His oracular shrine was at Delphi, where the beehive-shaped Omphalos Stone was revered as the navel of the world.

When Apollo first came to Delphi, the cleft in the rock there was guarded by a ferocious serpent, the python, which Apollo shot dead with his bow. The oracular priestess of the temple was then named the Pythia, who uttered her frequently double-edged and obscure prophecies in a trance, perhaps under the influence of hallucinogenic vapours that seeped through fissures in the rock into her underground chamber. The oracle at Delphi was rivalled for importance only by the oracle of Zeus at Dodona.

Python ab Apolline interficitur.

Artemis

Virgin huntress and mistress of all wild things, Artemis was the twin sister of Apollo. Their father was Zeus and their mother Leto, who often hunted with Artemis. The twins were archers, and Artemis spent most of her time hunting, accompanied by her band of nymphs, who were all sworn to chastity. When the nymph Callisto was raped by Zeus, her punishment was to be turned into a bear, some say by Artemis, others Hera.

Artemis did have some male followers, notably Hippolytus, the son of Theseus, and the giant hunter, Orion. Orion boasted there was no animal he could not kill, so the earth goddess Gaia sent a gigantic scorpion to sting him to death. At the pleading of Artemis and Leto, Orion was transformed into a constellation. Another famous hunter, Actaeon, grandson of Cadmus the king of Thebes, suffered a terrible fate when he chanced upon the naked Artemis bathing with her nymphs in a forest pool. By splashing water on him, the goddess turned him into a deer; he was then chased and torn to pieces by his own hounds.

Athena

The virgin goddess Athena was both a fearsome goddess of war and the goddess of crafts, such as spinning, weaving, carpentry and pottery. She was worshipped in various forms, notably as the goddess of victory, Athena Nike, and as the protectress of Athens, Athena Polias. Although, in the Trojan War, Athena was on the side of the Greeks, she was also regarded as the protectress of Troy. She is depicted in *The Odyssey* as the faithful friend and adviser of Odysseus, helping him throughout his long voyage home from Troy (see pages 132–4). Athena was also noted for her wisdom and intelligence, and is often shown accompanied by an owl.

Athena's birth was most unusual. When Zeus's first wife, Metis, was pregnant with her, Zeus learned that his wife's next child would be a son who would be king of gods and men. To prevent this, Zeus swallowed Metis. When it then came time for Athena to be born, Hephaestos split Zeus's head open with an axe, and Athena sprang out, fully armed and yelling her war cry.

Arachne's web

Arachne was an ordinary girl from Lydia, with an extraordinary skill: she was an excellent weaver. Proud of her work, Arachne challenged the goddess of weaving, Athena, to a contest. Athena disguised herself as an old woman and advised Arachne to take back her words, but this only spurred her on.

Athena wove the story of the rivalry between herself and Poseidon as to who should be the protector of the city of Athens. She added scenes from the punishment of those who dared to challenge the gods. Arachne wove scenes of the gods' disreputable behaviour: Zeus seducing Leda in the form of a swan and Danae as a shower of gold; Poseidon taking the shape of a stallion to make love to the goddess, Demeter; and Dionysos tricking Erigone by turning himself into a bunch of grapes. All of this was rendered so perfectly, it almost seemed real; Athena could find no fault. Enraged, she beat Arachne with a shuttle. When Arachne tried to hang herself, the goddess turned her into a spider, doomed to weave her perfect webs for all eternity.

The agony of Arachne in the underworld, as pictured by Gustave Doré illustrating Dante's *Inferno*.

Hades and
the underworld

Hades was the god of the cold, dark underworld, also commonly called Hades. Hermes, the messenger god, accompanied the dead to the river Acheron, where Charon the ferryman would row them across for the payment of one *obol*, a small coin usually left in the mouth of the dead.

The gates of the underworld were guarded by the three-headed dog Cerberus, who welcomed the shades (spirits of the dead) with a wagging tail, but would attack them if they tried to leave. In the underworld, a few shades lived in bliss in Elysium, some suffered in torment in Tartaros, while most gathered listlessly in the meadows of Asphodel. When the legendary hero, Odysseus, sought advice from the dead, he sarificed a sheep at the edge of the underworld, and the blood enabled them to speak; Achilles told him he would rather be a living serf than king of the dead. Although the dead had the appearance of living beings, they were insubstantial; Odysseus tried to embrace his mother's shade, but his arms closed on nothingness.

Ancient graffito of three-headed Cerberus, guardian of the gates of the underworld

The rape of Persephone

Persephone, also called the maiden Kore, was the daughter of Zeus and the corn goddess Demeter. One day when she was gathering flowers in a meadow, the earth opened and Hades, god of the underworld, drove out in his golden chariot and seized her. Persephone cried out in protest, calling for her father, but Zeus was receiving sacrifices in his temple of prayers and did not hear her. From the tops of the mountains to the depths of the sea, her cries reverberated around the earth, and this time her mother Demeter heard her. The sound pierced right through Demeter's heart and she let out her own great wail of grief. It was too late.

Hades carried the shrieking Persephone down, to be his bride in the chilly darkness of the underworld. Outraged that Zeus should have allowed this, Demeter cut herself off from the gods. She wandered the world in the guise of an old woman, and for a whole year the land lay barren. The gods pleaded with her to return, but she would not.

The Mysteries of Eleusis

When the corn goddess Demeter left the world barren in her grief, Zeus sent Hermes down to Hades to ask him to release her daughter Persephone, whom he had stolen to be his bride. Hades agreed, but first Persephone had to eat some pomegranate seeds. Because she had eaten in the land of the dead, Persephone was tied to it. She had to spend the winter in the underworld; for the rest of the year she was restored to her mother, who in turn renewed the fertility of the world.

Demeter founded a temple to her daughter at Eleusis, which became the centre of a religious cult thought 'to hold the entire human race together'. The Mysteries of Eleusis were sacred rites that took place every spring and autumn, to mark the arrival of Persephone and her return to Hades after the harvest. Initiates experienced a series of revelations promising new life after death, and learned of the birth in the fires of the underworld of a miraculous son to Persephone, named Brimos, the Strong One.

Eleusinian votive plaque

Dionysos

The god of wine and ecstasy was born twice. Zeus mated with Persephone in the form of a snake, and Zagreus was born, to be his heir. Hera urged the Titans to abduct the child. They tore him to pieces and ate everything but the heart, which Zeus implanted in his mortal lover Semele. Hera persuaded Semele to ask Zeus to appear to her in all his glory; when he did, she was burned to ash. Zeus snatched the baby from her womb and sewed it into his own thigh, from where Dionysos was born in due course.

Myths about Dionysos are often lighthearted, such as the story of the pirates who kidnapped him, only to be turned into dolphins. But worshippers of Dionysos worked themselves up into a divine frenzy; his female followers, the maenads, captured wild animals, tore them to pieces and ate them. When King Pentheus, son of Semele's sister Agave, tried to stamp out the worship of Dionysos, the god drove him mad. Spying on the secret rites, Pentheus was captured and torn apart by maenads. Dionysos was married to Ariadne.

Orpheus and Eurydice

Orpheus was the greatest singer, whose music could tame wild beasts or calm the seas. He was the son of the muse Calliope and Oiagros (or the god Apollo). He married the nymph Eurydice, but walking in the meadows after the ceremony she was bitten by a snake and died. Overcome with grief, Orpheus followed Eurydice to the underworld.

Orpheus begged Hades to allow Eurydice to live out her life. Eurydice, still limping from the snake bite, was allowed to leave, on the condition that Orpheus did not look back until both were out of the underworld. The path was dark, silent and steep and Eurydice limped on behind her husband. Worried, Orpheus turned back, and the nymph evaporated in his arms. Orpheus refused to take another woman, and stayed in his grove playing and singing to the animals, birds, trees and rocks. When he rejected the women of Thrace, they tore him to death. His head and lyre floated down the river Hebrus, still singing and playing. In the fields of the blessed, Orpheus was at last reunited with Eurydice.

Orpheus plays his lyre for the birds and animals.

The labours of Herakles

The greatest Greek hero, Herakles, was the son of Zeus by Alcmene. Jealous Hera drove him mad, and in a frenzy he killed his wife, Megara, and their children. As punishment, he was set twelve impossible tasks, or 'labours'.

He had to kill the ferocious Nemean lion; destroy the many-headed Hydra, which grew two new heads for every one lopped off; snare the sacred Ceryneian hind; capture the Erymanthian boar; clean out decades of dung from the stables of King Augeas; clear Lake Stymphalus of the monstrous birds that roosted there; capture Poseidon's bull, the father of the Minotaur; tame the man-eating mares of Diomedes; steal the girdle of Hippolyta, queen of the female warriors, the Amazons; and steal a herd of cattle from the giant Geryon. Then he was sent to steal the golden apples of the Hesperides. Lastly, Herakles had to capture Cerberus, the three-headed dog that guarded the underworld. This cleansed him of his guilt. After his death, Herakles was granted immortality among the gods.

Theseus
and the Minotaur

The Athenian hero, Theseus, was the son either of Aegeus, king of Athens, or of the sea god Poseidon, both of whom are said to have slept with his mother, Aethra, on the same night.

Every nine years, Athens paid a tribute of fourteen young men and women to King Minos of Crete. They served as food for the Minotaur, a beast with a bull's head and a man's body, who was the child of Minos's wife Pasiphae and a bull sent by Poseidon. The Minotaur's lair was an impenetrable labyrinth designed by the craftsman Daedalus. Intending to slay the Minotaur, Theseus volunteered to be part of the tribute. On Crete, Minos's daughter Ariadne fell in love with the hero, and helped him navigate the labyrinth. She tied a ball of twine at its entrance, so that he could retrace his path after killing the beast. On the way home, Theseus abandoned Ariadne on the island of Naxos. As his ship approached Athens, he forgot to hoist a white sail – a promise he'd made to Aegeus to show he was alive; thinking Theseus lost, his father leapt to his death in the Aegean Sea below.

Daedalus and Icarus

King Minos of Crete employed a genius artificer called Daedalus, who learned his skills from the goddess Athena. Daedalus constructed Talos, a giant bull-headed warrior of bronze, who guarded the island of Crete. When enemy fleets approached the coast, Talos would set them afire with the heat from his metal body.

When his wife Pasiphae gave birth to the half-man, half-bull Minotaur, Minos commanded Daedalus to contrive a gigantic labyrinth next to the palace at Knossos, to contain the creature. After the Minotaur was killed by Theseus, Minos imprisoned Daedalus and his son Icarus in a high tower. They gathered feathers from birds and built themselves wings with which to escape. Hoping for a closer look at Apollo in his fiery sun chariot, Icarus flew too high, falling to his death when the sun melted the wax holding the feathers of his wings. Daedalus took refuge with King Cocalus in Sicily. King Minos pursued him there, but Daedalus used his invention of hot-water pipes to scald him to death.

The Gorgons

The three Gorgons – Euryale, Stheno and Medusa – were hideous female creatures with golden wings and tusks like boars; their glances could turn men to stone. Euryale and Stheno were immortal, but Medusa was not. Athena had turned Medusa's lovely hair into a writhing mass of snakes, as punishment for sleeping with the sea god Poseidon in her temple.

When King Polydectes of Seriphos invited Perseus, the son of Zeus and Danae, to dinner the hero vowed to bring Medusa's head to the king as a gift. The gods aided him: nymphs brought Perseus winged sandals and a bag; Hades lent him his helmet of invisibility; Hermes gave him an adamantine sickle; and Athena lent him her shield of polished bronze. By observing the Gorgons in the mirrored shield Perseus waited until the sisters were asleep. He cut off Medusa's head using the sickle and stuffed it into his bag. From Medusa's severed neck were born two children by Poseidon, the winged horse Pegasus and Chrysaor. Perseus used the helmet of invisibility and the winged sandals to escape vengeance.

Perseus and Andromeda

On his way home from slaying the Gorgon Medusa, Perseus came to Ethiopia, where he saw a beautiful maiden chained to a rock on the shoreline. This was Andromeda, the daughter of King Kepheus. Her parents had boasted that she was more beautiful than the Nereids (the sea nymphs) and the sea god Poseidon was so enraged that he flooded the land with salt water. To pacify him, the Ethiopians agreed to sacrifice Andromeda to a sea monster.

Seeing her in chains, Perseus fell in love with Andromeda. Kepheus told him he could marry her, but he would have to save her first. Perseus used his winged sandals to rise up in the air and attack the sea monster from above with his sickle of adamant. Once the monster was dead, the hero claimed Andromeda as his bride. Kepheus's brother Phineus challenged Perseus, because Andromeda was already promised to him. When it seemed Phineus and his men might overwhelm him in battle, Perseus drew Medusa's head from its bag and turned them all to stone.

Oedipus and the sphinx

Oedipus was the son of Laius, king of Thebes, and Jocasta, his queen. It had been prophesied that, should Laius have a son, that son would kill him. So the baby was given to a herdsman, to be left on Mount Cithaeron to die. The softhearted herdsman gave the baby to another shepherd, who took him back to Corinth, where he was raised as the son of the king and queen.

The Delphic oracle told Oedipus he was destined to kill his father and marry his mother. Rather than stay in Corinth, he headed for Thebes. At a crossroads a man in a chariot tried to force him off the road and Oedipus killed him; this was Laius. Oedipus found Thebes ravaged by a man-eating sphinx. Jocasta's brother Creon, now ruling the city, decreed that whoever killed the sphinx would marry Jocasta and become king. Oedipus answered the riddle of the sphinx and killed it. Then, unknowingly, he married his mother. When plague befell the city, Oedipus's true identity was revealed. Horrified, Jocasta hanged herself and Oedipus blinded himself, henceforth to wander the world as an outcast.

Antigone

Antigone was one of four children born when Oedipus unwittingly married his mother Jocasta. She had a timid sister Ismene and two brothers, Eteocles and Polyneices. Antigone was known for her devotion to her family – a theme that Sophocles chose to explore in his play, *Antigone*.

The play opens with Eteocles and Polyneices, rivals for the rulership of Thebes, killing each other in fulfilment of their father's curse. Their uncle Creon, assuming rulership, buries Eteocles, but declares that Polyneices, the attacker, should remain unburied on the plain, to be eaten by the birds. Antigone defies her uncle, and scatters earth on her brother's body in a token burial. She is walled alive in a tomb as punishment. Creon's son Haemon (her lover) and the seer Teiresias plead for clemency. Creon, convinced by Teiresias that he has angered the gods, relents. He stops on his way to bury Polyneices, and by the time he arrives at the tomb, Antigone has hanged herself. Haemon kills himself, as does his mother Eurydice. Creon is left alone with his bitter regrets.

The Judgement of Paris

Paris was the son of Priam and Hecuba, king and queen of Troy. The goddesses Hera, Athena and Aphrodite – spurred into rivalry by the goddess of strife, Eris – asked Paris to judge who was the most beautiful. As rewards, Hera offered him power, Athena pledged victory in battle, and Aphrodite promised him the beautiful Helen, wife of the Spartan king Menelaos. Paris chose Aphrodite and abducted Helen, sparking the ten-year Trojan War.

Fighting on the Trojan side, Paris was regarded as inferior to his more warlike brother, Hector. Early on, he fought Menelaos in single combat, and was defeated. Aphrodite had to rescue him, and summoned Helen to his bed. While they were making love, Agamemnon, the leader of the Greek forces, announced that Menelaos had clearly triumphed and that, if the Trojans returned Helen and paid compensation, the war would be over. But the gods did not allow it. Hera was implacable in her desire to see Troy destroyed. Athena persuaded one of the Trojans to break the truce by firing an arrow at Menelaos, and the war was rekindled.

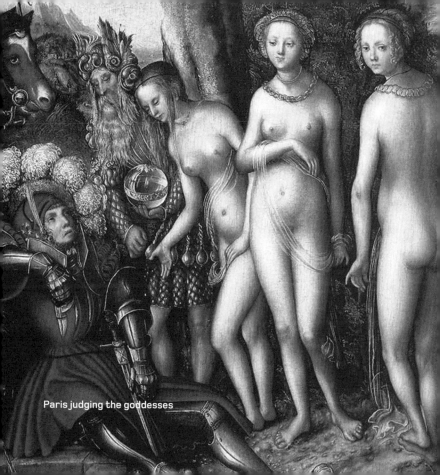

Paris judging the goddesses

Achilles

Achilles was the son of King Peleus and the sea nymph Thetis. Thetis tried to make their baby immortal by anointing him with ambrosia by day and placing him in the embers of the fire at night. A later version of the story has Thetis dipping the baby into the river Styx in Hades; she holds him by his heel, and this part of his body remains vulnerable.

Achilles was the greatest of the Greek warriors in the Trojan War, but he quarrelled with the leader Agamemnon for taking his slave girl, Briseis. As Achilles sulked in his tent, refusing to fight, the tide of war turned against the Greeks. The hero lent his armour to his friend Patroclus, who was killed by the Trojan prince Hector. Achilles returned to the field, slaughtering many Trojans, including Hector. He tied the corpse to a chariot by its ankles and dragged it around the city walls for eleven days. King Priam pleaded for the return of his son's body and Achilles relented. Achilles was later killed by an arrow in his heel, shot by Hector's brother Paris and guided by the god Apollo.

Achilles binds the wounds of Patroclus.

The Trojan Horse

In the Trojan War, the Greek forces overwhelmed the Trojans, but could not breach the city's impenetrable walls. Odysseus, king of Ithaca, tried to avoid joining the Greeks by pretending to be mad, but he was forced to go, leaving his wife Penelope and baby son Telemachus behind. The hero's importance to the Greeks lay in his wily intelligence and his eloquence rather than in his military might.

It was Odysseus who uncovered the oracles that told how Troy might be taken. One of them required Odysseus and Diomedes to enter Troy and steal the Palladium, the sacred image of Athena, guardian of the city, from her temple. Odysseus devised the ploy of the Trojan Horse – an enormous wooden horse that was left outside the gates of Troy as a gift from the Greeks, who had supposedly sailed away. The Trojans dragged the horse inside the city, debating what to do with it. At night, Odysseus and the other warriors hidden inside the hollow body of the horse crept out and slaughtered the city's inhabitants. This gave rise to the proverb: beware of Greeks bearing gifts.

Scenes from the Trojan War

The Odyssey

After the Trojan War, the Greek heroes returned to their homes. For Odysseus, this was to prove a ten-year journey full of peril and adventure. The hero won the enmity of the sea god Poseidon by blinding his son, the Cyclops Polyphemus. He spent a year with the enchantress Circe, who turned all his men into pigs. And he visited Hades to consult the seer Teiresias.

Before reaching home, Odysseus had to endure the song of the Sirens, whose singing lured sailors to their doom; he also had to pass between the sea monster Scylla and the whirlpool Charybdis. Zeus wrecked the Greeks' ships in revenge for stealing the cattle of the sun god Helios; only Odysseus survived. Shipwrecked on the island of the nymph Calypso, he spent seven years as her consort, but rejected her offer to make him immortal, preferring to return to his wife, Penelope. When, at last, he reached Ithaca, he found his wife besieged by suitors. Disguised as a beggar, recognized only by his faithful dog, Odysseus drew his great bow and slaughtered them.

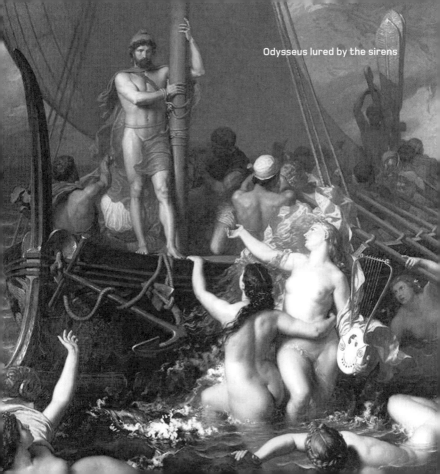
Odysseus lured by the sirens

The Golden Fleece

The story of Jason and the Argonauts is a classic quest for a fabled treasure – a magical Golden Fleece guarded by a sleepless dragon. The fleece was in the possession of Aeetes, the king of Colchis. Aeetes promised the fleece to Jason, son of the king of Iolcos, if he could plough a field with fire-breathing bulls, sow the ground with dragon's teeth and kill the host of armed men who sprang from the earth.

Jason succeeded, with Medea's help. Medea was Aeetes's daugther; Aphrodite had made her fall in love with Jason. She took Jason to the sacred grove of Ares, lulled the dragon to sleep and enabled Jason to steal the fleece. The hero gave the fleece to King Pelias, who had taken his father's throne and hoped he would not survive the quest. Medea persuaded Pelias's daughters to kill their father, pretending she could make him young again. Jason and Medea then fled to Corinth, where they had two sons. When Jason deserted her, Medea killed both his new bride and their two sons, to inflict the maximum pain on him.

Jason delivering the fleece to King Pelias

King Midas

Midas was king of Phrygia. Recognizing an old drunk as the satyr Silenus, companion of Dionysos, Midas entertained him royally, and in return Dionysos granted him a wish. Midas wished that everything he touched should turn to gold. And so it did – including his daughter. Soon the desperate king was begging Dionysos to remove the gift. The god told him to bathe in the river Pactolus, which washed away his golden touch, turning the sands of the river golden ever after.

Later, Midas witnessed a musical contest between the gods Apollo and Pan, judged by the mountain god Tmolus. When Tmolus awarded the prize to Apollo, Midas objected, saying that Pan deserved it. Apollo cursed Midas with asses' ears. The king kept his shameful ears covered up, but could not hide them from his barber who, sworn to secrecy, simply had to share what he knew. He dug a hole in the ground and whispered the secret into it. A bed of reeds grew there, and every time the wind blew through them, they too whispered, 'King Midas has asses' ears.'

Myths of ancient Rome

Roman mythology incorporates the myths of ancient Greece, but the overlap is far from perfect. This is because Roman myth represents a complex web of cults and rituals, with a cast of major and minor gods drawn from various other cultures besides Greek, including Etruscan, Latin and Syrian.

The Romans had a practical attitude to divinity, adding deities as required. A temple, such as the Pantheon in Rome, could be dedicated to 'all the gods'; equally, a shrine might honour 'the unknown god'. The Capitoline Triad of Jupiter, Juno and Minerva represents a way of worshipping a threefold divinity that derives from Etruscan culture. Chiming with Egyptian practice, it bears no relation to ancient Greek mythology. Often, north Italian deities were assimilated with Greek gods: the goddess of hunting, Diana, merged with Greek Artemis, and Mercury, the god of trade and finance, merged with the Greek messenger god Hermes. Some Roman gods came directly from Greece. Apollo, for example, has no early Italian equivalent as god of the sun and of music.

Diana, Roman goddess of the hunt and nature

Dido and Aeneas

The founding father of Rome was Aeneas, a Trojan prince who escaped the sack of Troy bearing many of its treasures. Among them, the Romans believed, was the Palladium, a statue of the virgin goddess Pallas Athena.

Aeneas was said to be the son of the Roman goddess Venus, but her patronage was balanced by the enmity of the goddess Juno. When Aeneas set out with his fleet to found a new Troy in Italy, Juno asked Aeolus, god of the winds, to wreck the ships off the coast of Carthage. There, Venus ensured that Aeneas and Dido, queen of Carthage, fell in love with each other. Trapped in a cave during a violent storm, the couple consummated their love, and Aeneas forgot all about his original quest. But Jupiter, king of the gods, sent messenger god Mercury to remind him, and to urge him to continue on his journey. When Dido discovered that Aeneas planned to leave her, she built a sacrificial pyre; as his ship set sail from Carthage, Dido stabbed herself with his sword and leapt into the flames.

Aeneas and the Sibyl of Cumae

When Aeneas landed in Italy, he consulted a prophetess, the Sibyl of Cumae, who guarded an entrance to the underworld. He begged for her help, wanting to see his father Anchises again. She told him to pluck the Golden Bough, which grew in the woods nearby, as a present for Proserpina (in Greek: Persephone). Shown the Golden Bough, Charon the ferryman agreed to take Aeneas and the Sibyl across the river Styx. The Sibyl drugged the guard dog Cerberus, and they entered the land of the dead.

Aeneas saw his lover Dido there, but she turned away without a word. He found his father by the river Lethe; souls who are to be reborn drink from the river to forget their past lives. Three times Aeneas tried to embrace his father, but his arms closed on empty air. Anchises then prophesied the founding of Rome and a roll of future Roman heroes. Aeneas and the Sibyl returned from the underworld via the gate of ivory through which the Manes, or spirits of the dead, send false dreams. True dreams were sent through the gate of horn.

The Cumaean Sibyl

Romulus and Remus

Romulus and Remus were the twin sons of Aeneas's descendant Rhea Silvia, a Vestal Virgin, who was raped by Mars, the god of war. At their birth, their mother's wicked uncle Amulius, who had usurped her father's throne in Alba Longa, killed her and threw the twins into the river Tiber. The river god carried them safely to the shore, and a she-wolf suckled them in the Lupercal Cave until they were found by Faustulus, a shepherd, who raised them.

Mars appeared to the twins when they were older and told them their history. They killed Amulius and restored their grandfather to the throne. The twins then decided to build a new city on the Tiber. Romulus claimed that the gods favoured him and began to plough a furrow to mark the city's limits. When Remus jeered at him and sacrilegiously jumped over the furrow Romulus killed him. Once the city was established, Mars took Romulus away in his chariot, to become a god. The festival of purification known as Lupercalia was a ritual race around the boundary first ploughed by Romulus.

The ruling gods

The ruling gods of Rome were the Capitoline Triad: Jupiter, Juno and Minerva. Temples, called Capitolia, dedicated to these three gods were built all over the Roman Empire, but the chief one was on the Capitoline Hill at Rome.

Jupiter was the ruler of the gods and Juno was his wife. In the Capitolium they were worshipped as Jupiter Optimus Maximus (Jupiter Best and Greatest) and as Juno Regina (Juno the Queen), and it is easy to understand why they would be regarded as important. But why Minerva, goddess of handicrafts, wisdom and war? Although identified with the Greek gods Zeus, Hera and Athena, the Capitoline Triad reflected the ruling triad of the Etruscans, the indigenous people of central Italy, which consisted of Tinia, the ruler of the heavens, Uni, his wife, goddess of the cosmos, and Menvra, goddess of wisdom and war, who was born from the head of Tinia. Tinia (Thunderer) was renamed Diospiter or Jupiter by the Romans, and only after conquering Greece did they assimilate these three ruling gods into the Greek pantheon.

Mars, god of war

The war god Mars was born to Juno after Flora, the goddess of spring, touched her with a magic herb. Mars started out as an Etruscan god of agriculture. He was married to the goddess of valour Nerio, sometimes identified with Bellona, goddess of war. Jupiter, Mars and Quirinus were the most important gods of early Rome. Quirinus was a Sabine god of war and was identified with the deified Romulus, who was the son of Mars. In his original role, Mars was venerated as 'Father Mars', but over time he acquired the warlike characteristics of Quirinus. Mars once begged the aged goddess Anna Perenna to help him seduce the virgin goddess Minerva. Anna played along, but took Minerva's place herself, and only when Mars lifted her veil did he discover the trick.

In the month of March, the leaping priests of Mars danced with spears and shields to banish evil spirits who had entered the city in the winter, and to ensure an abundant harvest. This festival also ushered in a new summer season of warfare from March to October.

Vesta, goddess of the hearth

The virgin goddess of the hearth and family, Vesta guarded her virtue closely. Priapus, the god of fertility and sexuality, came upon her as she slept one night and was filled with desire. The virtuous goddess was saved by the braying of a donkey that was grazing nearby.

Romans worshipped Vesta in their homes but there was also a circular temple of Vesta in the Forum, the heart of Rome. The Vestal Virgins were Rome's only female priesthood, and played a key role in all kinds of rituals and ceremonies. Tending the fire of Vesta, said to have been brought from Troy by Aeneas, was their most important task; the fire was ceremonially renewed every New Year's Day. The chastity of the Vestal Virgins was essential to the health and safety of Rome itself — if lost, the city itself was besmirched. The offending Vestal was buried alive, with a few days' meagre rations, so that her blood was not spilled; her eventual death was by the will of the Manes, the underworld gods.

Bona Dea,
the good goddess

One of the most important and revered of all Roman deities was the women's goddess, Bona Dea. She was identified with another Roman goddess, Fauna, who was either daughter or wife to the pastoral god Faunus. One myth tells how Faunus fell in love with his daughter, but she rejected him, even after he got her drunk with wine. He beat her with sticks of myrtle before having intercourse with her in the form of a snake. A variant of this story makes Fauna the wife of Faunus, who beat her to death with sticks of myrtle as punishment for getting drunk. In either event, she then became the goddess Bona Dea.

As a victim of domestic abuse, Bona Dea was regarded by women as the goddess who listened, so altars were dedicated to her ears. Men were completely excluded from both her temple and her cult. The festival of Bona Dea was held in the house of the chief magistrate. His wife led the women-only ceremony, assisted by the Vestal Virgins. Wine drunk in Bona Dea's honour was referred to as milk.

The goddess Cybele, the great mother

Cybele was an Anatolian goddess of fertility and mother of all living things, whose worship spread from her sanctuary on Mount Dindymus in Phrygia, first to Greece and then to Rome. The Romans called her Magna Mater, the Great Mother; The poets Virgil and Ovid both called her the mother of the gods. A Phrygian youth named Attis won the heart of Cybele through the purity of his love, and she asked him to guard her shrine and to promise to remain a virgin. When Attis broke his promise by seducing the wood nymph Sagaritis, the enraged goddess cut down the nymph's tree, killing her. Attis went mad and cut off his genitals, an act replicated by the priests of Cybele, who castrated themselves in order to serve the goddess. In 204 BCE, in accordance with a prophecy from the ancient Greek Sibylline books, the sacred black stone that represented the goddess was brought to Rome, and a temple built for her on the Palatine Hill. Her cult, with its ecstatic worship, spread all over the empire; under Emperor Claudius, worship of Cybele became part of Rome's state religion.

Mithras, the bull slayer

Mithras was the focus of a male-only mystery cult that promised new life after death, and was particularly followed by Roman soldiers. He was worshipped as the cosmic ruler of cave-like underground temples called 'mithraea'. As it was a mystery religion with initiates sworn to secrecy, we do not know precisely the myth behind it. The only certain detail is that Mithras slays a bull, probably symbolizing the constellation Perseus 'slaying' the constellation Taurus and ushering in a new age. Mithras was identified with Perseus and, like Perseus killing Medusa (see page 120), Mithras always looks away as he slays the bull. Pictorial carvings seem to depict the underlying myth that creation is under threat from a drought caused by the forces of evil. A new god, Mithras, arises from a rock to take control of the cosmos. He shoots an arrow and a spring gushes out to relieve the world's thirst. Then he catches a bull that has been absorbing all the moisture from the moon, drags the creature into a cave and sacrifices it. Animals come to drink its blood and trees begin to branch and bear leaves and fruit.

Myths of the Celts

The myths of the Celts in Iron Age Europe were never written down, and only survive in names of deities and the occasional visual representations. For example, the Gundestrup Cauldron depicts the horned Celtic god Cernunnos as Lord of the Beasts. It was only in Ireland that anything resembling a coherent Celtic mythology was recorded; a collection of Welsh myths known as The Mabinogion are more muddled.

One of the deities who appears on numerous inscriptions from the Celtic world is Sucellus. He carries a hammer, with which he may have struck the earth in spring to waken it from its winter sleep, and a pot or cauldron, a symbol of nourishment, rebirth and resurrection. The Hwicce of southwest England regarded themselves as the people of 'the goddess of the sacred vessel' – a vessel equated with the valleys of the landscape, a Grail-like cauldron of plenty, and the womb of the Great Goddess. Magical cauldrons are a constant theme in Celtic myth, right up to the Arthurian quest for the Holy Grail.

Depiction of Cernunnos on the Gundestrup Cauldron from Denmark

The Daghda

The Daghda, leader of a super race known as the Tuatha Dé Danaan, is the Irish equivalent of the continental Celtic god of the weather and the harvest, Sucellus (the Good Striker), who carried a hammer and a pot or cauldron. The Daghda (the Good God) carried a huge club; one end of this club killed the living, while the other revived the dead. His cauldron (the archetype of the Holy Grail) was the source of an inexhaustible supply of food.

The wife of Sucellus was Nantosuelta (the Winding River). The Daghda, too, fell in love with a river, Boann, the spirit of the river Boyne. She was already married to Elcmar or Nechtan (both of these names seeming to represent Nuadu of the Silver Arm, an earlier king of the Tuatha Dé Danaan, disqualified from kingship by his missing arm). The Daghda sent Elcmar away on an errand, then spelled the sun to stand still in the sky for nine months, so that the child he had with Boann was both conceived and born on the same day. This child was Angus mac Óc, who was famous for helping star-crossed lovers.

Cuchulain

The Ulster hero Cuchulain was the son of Deichtine, either by the sun god Lugh or by her brother, King Conchobar of Ulster. Cuchulain was Ulster's champion in the Cattle Raid of Cooley, a great conflict between Connaught and Ulster caused by Queen Medb of Connaught stealing Conchobar's prized bull. In fact, he fought alone in a series of single combats, as all Conchobar's warriors were struck down by a mysterious weakness.

Cuchulain fought in a battle frenzy, performing his famous 'salmon leap' and wielding a fearsome spear and sword. At a ford, he fought against his foster-brother Ferdiad for four days before killing him, and then singing a lament over his body. At last Cuchulain was speared in his stomach by Lugaid. Realizing he had been dealt his death blow, Cuchulain tied himself to a standing stone using his belt, so that he could continue fighting to the end. When the war goddess Morrigan landed on his shoulder in the form of a crow, his time was up, and Lugaid ran him through.

The death of Cuchulain

Deirdre of the Sorrows

Deirdre, one of the most famous figures in Irish myth, was the daughter of King Conchobar's chief storyteller. When she was born, the druid Cathbhadh prophesied that she would be a great beauty and would bring disaster to the people of Ulster.

King Conchobar insisted that when she was grown he would marry her. Deirdre had a vision of her ideal lover, with hair as black as a raven's, cheeks as red as blood and skin as white as snow. It was Naoise, Conchobar's nephew. The two eloped to Scotland, where they lived happily for many years, until an offer of amnesty from Conchobar lured them back to Ireland. But it was a trick and Conchobar had Naoise killed by a warrior, Eóghan. Deirdre was taken to Conchobar, but gave him no joy, never smiling or raising her head. Asked what she hated most, she answered, 'Eóghan', so Conchobar gave her to him; she leapt to her death from his chariot. Many of Conchobar's warriors deserted him and fought against him in the Cattle Raid of Cooley, thus fulfilling Cathbhadh's prophecy.

The voyage of Bran

The voyage of Bran is one of many mystery voyages in Celtic myth. Lured by a magical apple branch, Bran set out in search of the otherworld where there was neither illness nor death. After two days, he and his men met Manannan, god of the sea, riding across the waves in his chariot. He told them of the wonders of the ocean and its many magical islands.

The first island Bran came to was the Island of Joy, from which the sound of laughter filled the sky. One of his men begged to go ashore, and as soon as his feet touched the land he started laughing too, and would not return to the boat. Then Bran came to the Isle of Women, where the beautiful inhabitants invited them ashore, and they lived in perfect bliss for a year. One of Bran's men, Nechtan, was homesick, and persuaded the others to take him back to Ireland. The women told the others on no account to set foot on Irish soil. When Nechtan leapt from the boat, his body turned to dust – they had been away centuries, not months. So Bran set back out to sea, for ever.

Statue of Manannan, god of the sea, at Gortmore View Point, Limavady, Ireland

Finn Mac Cumhail

Finn Mac Cumhail (Finn MacCool), leader of the band of warriors known as the Fianna, was the hero of thousands of tales in both manuscript and oral tradition. Finn possessed the legendary crane-skin bag made by the sea god Manannan, which contained many treasures including his father's spear, helmet and shield. Finn also had magical wisdom, acquired when he was a child studying with Finnegas the bard. Finnegas caught the Salmon of Knowledge, and gave it to Finn to cook. Finn burned his thumb on the fish and, putting it in his mouth, gained supernatural wisdom. Many and varied, Finn's adventures often involved matching himself against creatures of the otherworld, such as a supernatural boar. He is also said to have laid the Giant's Causeway between Ireland and Scotland in order to fight a Scottish giant, Far Rua. His heroism was marred in old age by his jealous pursuit of Diarmaid, his rival in love for a young beauty, Gráinne. When, with Finn's connivance, Diarmaid was gored by a magical boar, Finn refused to heal him. Finn was disgraced, and his men abandoned him.

Finn Mac Cumhail is said to have created the Giant's Causeway.

Oísin and the land of youth

Oísin was the son of the legendary hero Finn Mac Cumhail. His mother was caught by Finn in the form of a deer and disenchanted, but later turned back into a deer again.

Oísin fell in love with Niamh of the Golden Hair, the daughter of the king of Tír na n'Óg, the land of eternal youth. After many adventures with his father's men, the Fianna, Oísin headed westwards with Niamh on her white horse. When they arrived in Tír na n'Óg they made love for 300 years. Wanting to see his old home, Oísin decided to pay a visit to Ireland – Niamh warned him on no account to dismount from his horse. On arrival there, he found everything decayed. His father Finn was long dead, and his hall abandoned.

At Glenasmole in County Wicklow, Oísin passed some men trying to lift a heavy stone onto a wagon. Leaning down to help them, he slipped from his white horse. As soon as he touched the ground he became old, shrunken and blind.

Oísin departs with Niamh of the Golden Hair on her white steed.

Pwyll, prince of Dyfed

The story of Pwyll is told in the First Branch of The Mabinogion, a collection of Welsh myths. While out hunting, Pwyll, prince of Dyfed, saw a pack of strange hounds pursue and take down a deer. He drove the dogs off, and gave the deer to his own pack. A horseman appeared, who said he was Arawn, the king of Annwn, the underworld. He told Pwyll that, in order to atone for his behaviour, he must swap identities, bodies even, with Arawn for a year. Arawn oversaw Dyfed, while Pwyll ruled in Annwn, sleeping with Arawn's wife, but never making love to her. At the end of the year, Pwyll had to fight and kill Arawn's rival, Hafgan. Arawn warned him to strike just one blow; if he struck another, Hafgan would revive. For this Pwyll earned the title 'head of Annwn'.

Pwyll was married to Rhiannon, a magical figure who was either a fairy or a goddess. When their baby son Pryderi disappeared, Rhiannon was accused of infanticide. For this she was made to sit by a horse-block at the palace gate for seven years, offering to carry visitors on her back.

Rhiannon and Pryderi

The head of Brân

The Welsh hero Brân the Blessed was also known as Bendigeidfran, son of Llyr the sea god. He was a giant who owned a magical horn of plenty. His beautiful sister Branwen was given in marriage to the Irish king Matholwch.

Brân's half-brother Efnisien disapproved of Branwen's marriage and mutilated Matholwch's horses in his stable. As a result, Branwen was humiliated, made to work as a cook and was struck every day by the butcher. She managed to send a starling to Brân with a message, and he took an army to Ireland. The Irish had the advantage of a magic cauldron that brought dead soldiers back to life, but even so Brân prevailed.

By the end he had only seven men left and Brân himself was mortally wounded. He told his men to cut off his head and bury it at the White Mount in London, to protect Britain from invaders. King Arthur is said to have dug up the head so that Britain should rely solely on the valour of his knights.

Branwen takes comfort from her tame starling.

Blodeuwedd

Math fab Mathonwy, the king of Gwynedd, had to rest his feet in the lap of a virgin whenever he was not at war. His nephew Gwydion suggested his own sister Arianrhod. Math asked her to step over a magic wand to prove her virginity and, as she did so, she gave birth to two children. One was Dylan, son of the wave. The other was a shapeless lump, which Gwydion wrapped up and put in a chest until he heard screams. He opened up the chest to find a baby boy. This was Lleu Llaw Gyffes.

Arianrhod cursed Lleu never to have a human wife. Gwydion and Math, both of whom had magical powers, made a woman out of the flowers of the oak, broom and meadowsweet to be his wife. They named her Blodeuwedd. But Blodeuwedd betrayed Lleu with a nobleman, Gronw Pebr, and although Lleu was almost invulnerable they conspired to kill him. When struck by Gronw's spear, Lleu was transformed into an eagle. Gwydion found him, turned him back into a man and nursed him back to health. Lleu then killed Gronw and turned Blodeuwedd into an owl.

Lleu, in eagle form

Taliesin

The enchantress Ceridwen had a daughter, Creiwy, who was the most beautiful girl in the world. She also had a son, Avagddu, who was the ugliest boy.

Because Avagddu was so ugly, Ceridwen brewed a cauldron of inspiration and knowledge for him. She set a boy called Gwion to stir it for a year. On the last day, three drops splashed up and burned Gwion's finger. He put it in his mouth to soothe the pain, and immediately gained vision of past, present and future. Gwion fled, with Ceridwen pursuing. He changed into a hare, she to a greyhound; he to a fish, and she to an otter; he to a bird, and she to a hawk. He dived into a sheaf of wheat and became a golden grain; she became a black hen and swallowed him whole. Nine months later she gave birth to a boy so beautiful she could not kill him, but instead set him adrift in a leather bag. He was found by a prince named Elphin, who called him Taliesin ('radiant brow'). When grown, Taliesin used his magical inspiration to become the most famous bard in all Wales.

Ceridwen brewing the cauldron of inspiration

King Arthur

King Arthur was a mythical king of Britain, first mentioned in early Welsh poetry. In 'The Spoils of Annwn', attributed to the bard Taliesin, Arthur leads an expedition to a glass fortress in the underworld, in search of the 'cauldron of the chief of Annwn'. In the Middle Ages, this became the search for the Holy Grail.

From the 12th century, stories about King Arthur and his Knights of the Round Table spread across western Europe. The illegitimate son of King Uther Pendragon, Arthur proved he was the rightful king by drawing a sword from a block of stone, before establishing his court at Camelot. Arthur's wife Guinevere had an affair with his close friend, and greatest knight, Sir Lancelot. For this, Arthur banished Lancelot. Arthur's illegitimate son Mordred took advantage of the turmoil to launch a bid for the throne. At the Battle of Camlann, Arthur killed Mordred in single combat, but was himself fatally wounded. He sailed to the Isle of Avalon, where the apples of immortality grew, to die. Some legends say Arthur is sleeping, to wake with his knights in Britain's hour of need.

GAWAIN · BORY · LANCELOT · GALARD · PERSEVAL · LE ROY · ARTVS · DELIAS

LE ROY · RYOHS · LE ROY · CARADOS · LE ROY · LOIER · LE ROY · BANDE

The Holy Grail

At King Arthur's Round Table sat all the greatest knights in the world. But there was one chair that remained empty, the Siege Perilous, or seat of danger. The wizard Merlin prophesied that when it was filled, the days of the Round Table would draw to an end.

One day an unknown knight appeared and sat in the seat. Behind him the words 'Galahad, the High Prince' appeared in letters of gold. Galahad was the son of Sir Lancelot, by Elaine, the daughter of the crippled King Pelles. That night the knights had a vision of the Holy Grail in which Christ's blood was caught at the crucifixion. Sir Galahad announced a quest to find it. The knights scattered far and wide, but only three – Galahad, Perceval and Bors – found the Grail, in the castle of King Pelles, whereupon he was made whole and his blighted land bloomed again. At Mass, only Galahad, who was utterly pure in heart and soul, saw the Grail uncovered. He was subsumed in its light, and both Galahad and the Grail vanished from the world of men.

In Dante Gabriel Rosetti's 1874 painting, the Grail is presented by a maiden overlooked by the Holy Spirit in the form of a dove.

Myths of Scandinavia

The direct, brutal and comic Norse myths are the only surviving account of the mythologies developed across northern Europe in the Bronze Age, when the Great Mother goddess of the Stone Age is said to have given way to a powerful male Sky god, depicted with an axe or hammer in Scandinavian rock engravings. Such a god was Perun, the thunder god by whom the Slavs swore their oaths of peace and war. Woden, or Wotan, and Thunor, or Donar, were the chief gods of the Germanic peoples by the first century CE; as Odin and Thor they were also the chief gods of the Vikings, to whom sacrifices were made of goods, animals and humans. The Norse goddesses derive many characteristics from the earlier Danish fertility goddess, Nerthus. A very different, poetic and oblique mythology survived orally in Karelia (a region in present-day Russia and Finland), codified in the 19th century in the magical Finnish Kalevala, with its extraordinary cast of characters, such as Väinämöinen, who was born already old and sings the world into being; Tapio, the lord of the forest; and Louhi, the harsh mistress of the Northland.

Frontispiece of Snorri Sturluson's *Prose Edda*, a collection of poetry and Norse mythology, dated *c.* 1220

The Norse Creation

The Vikings believed that, in the beginning, there were two realms: one of ice and one of fire, separated by a chasm of creative potentiality, Ginnungagap. From Niflheim, the ice realm, rivers of poison flowed into the chasm and froze, while fiery sparks and burning winds flew from the fire realm of Muspell.

Where cold wind from the north met hot wind from the south, they shaped the poison ice into an hermaphroditic being – Ymir. While he slept, Ymir sweated, and two creatures, one male and one female, formed from the sweat in his left armpit. These were the first frost giants, the enemies of the gods. Ymir was nourished by a magical cow, Audhumla, also formed from the ice. The cow sustained herself by licking the salty poison rime. As she licked, she uncovered a male form, beautiful and strong. This was Buri, the grandfather of the first gods, Odin, Vili and Ve. They killed Ymir and created the cosmos, using his body to make the earth, his bones to make rocks, his blood to make the sea, his brains to make the clouds and his skull to make the sky.

Odin, Vili and Ve slay Ymir, the first being

War between the Aesir and the Vanir

There were two races of gods. One was the Aesir, with Odin at its head. The other was the Vanir, with Njord, god of the sea, at its head. The chief Vanir were Njord and his children Freyr and Freyja, fertility gods who make the world fruitful.

War between the two races came about because the Vanir were jealous of the gold-roofed halls raised by the Aesir in their home Asgard. They sent a sorceress named Gullveig (probably Freyja in disguise) to try to wheedle some gold from the Aesir. Offended, the Aesir burned Gullveig three times on a fire. Having the powers of a witch Gullveig came back to life each time. When she returned to the Vanir empty-handed, they attacked Asgard with spells and razed its walls. The war became so mutually destructive that the two sides arranged a truce and a hostage swap. Njord, Freyr and Freyja went to live with the Aesir, while slow-witted Honir and wise Mimir went to live with the Vanir. The Vanir, disappointed with their dull new leader Honir, cut off Mimir's head and sent it to Odin, who anointed and preserved it to retain its wisdom.

Gullveig is lifted over the fire.

Yggdrasil

At the centre of the Viking cosmos was Yggdrasil, the World Tree, a giant ash that held up the sky and sustained the world. The tree had three roots – one in Jotunheim, home of the giants; one in Asgard, home of the Aesir gods; and one in Niflheim, the realm of ice where Hel, land of the dead lay. Beneath each of these roots was a spring – Mimir's well of wisdom in Jotunheim; Urd's well of fate in Asgard; and Hvergelmir, the source of the poison that filled the chasm at the time of creation, in Niflheim.

Urd's well was guarded by the three Norns – Fate, Being and Necessity. These three shaped the lives of men and women from birth to death. They also watered the tree every day to keep it alive; drops of this water fell to the earth as refreshing dew. Yggdrasil needed such guardians, because it was constantly under attack. An evil dragon, Nidhogg, gnawed at its roots, along with other serpents. A giant eagle, Hraesvelg, sat at its tip, flapping its wings to create the wind. The squirrel Ratatoskr scampered up and down between the two, delivering insulting messages.

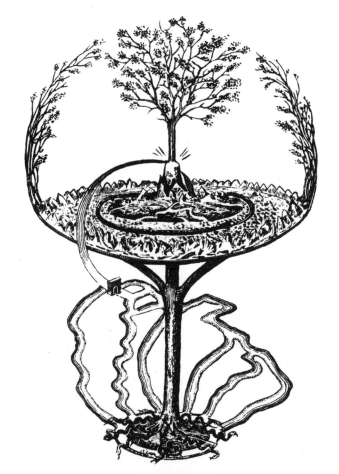

Odin and the runes

The All-Father of the Norse gods, Odin has many names and disguises. He was the god of battles, and of those who died in battle or sacrifice. (Those who drowned went to Ran, the sea goddess, while those who died of illness or old age went to Hel, goddess of the underworld, also called Hel.)

Odin was also the god of poetry, inspiration and magic. He was one-eyed, because he traded the other for a single mouthful from the well of wisdom. His most famous search for knowledge was when he sacrificed himself on Yggdrasil. He hung for nine nights on the windswept tree, pierced through the side with his spear Gungnir. At the end of the ordeal, Odin screamed out, and seized the magic runes that had been hidden in the branches. These runes were used for writing, but also for casting spells and for divination. Carving a rune three times carried a magical charge. Knowledge of the runes gave Odin many powers, such as healing, quelling flames or storms, re-animating corpses, and the ability to seduce any woman he wanted.

Norse goddesses

Most Norse myths tell of the exploits of the male gods, the Aesir. Yet the goddesses, the Asynjur, were regarded with equal importance. The Icelandic poet Snorri Sturluson wrote, 'No less holy are the Asynjur, nor is their power less.'

The highest of the Asynjur was Frigg, the wife of Odin, who knew all fates, but kept silent about them. Frigg has been identified as the goddess of love, but she does not really take this role in the myths. Freyja, a goddess who joined the Aesir from the Vanir, is more concerned with love and fertility, and was herself the object of desire from several giants. The daughter of the sea god Njord and his sister, Freyja seems originally to have been married to her brother Freyr, though later her husband is named as Od, who left her for so long she shed tears of gold. Freyja travels in a carriage drawn by cats, and possesses two great treasures – a falcon cloak and the gold necklace Brisingamen. The goddess Idun is guardian of the golden apples that keep the gods forever young.

The goddess Freyja rides in her carriage drawn by two cats.

Thor, the thunderer

There are more myths about Thor, the super-strong Norse god of thunder, than about Odin, the All-Father. Thor's weapon was the mighty hammer Mjollnir, which produced thunder and lightning, and always returned to Thor's hand. Viking wedding vows were made over hammers, and many Vikings wore small hammer amulets around their necks to gain the protection of Thor, especially on sea journeys.

Thor was the son of Odin, but Frigg was not his mother; instead he was said to be the son of the earth herself. Thor made many sorties in the land of the giants, often accompanied by the trickster god Loki. One myth tells how the giant Thrym stole Thor's hammer, but agreed to give it back in return for the goddess Freyja as his bride. Unwilling to meet these terms, Loki dressed Thor in bridal clothes and they set off to Jotunheim together. Thrym was delighted with his new bride. Fetching out the hammer, he laid it on the false Freyja's lap to sanctify the marriage. As soon as the hammer was within reach, Thor swung it and killed Thrym.

Loki, the trickster

The trickster Loki was a misfit among the gods. He did not belong to either the Aesir or the Vanir, but was a frost giant. His privileged position among the Aesir was due to his being Odin's foster brother. Loki's restless cunning nature saw him often get the gods either into or out of trouble. He acted out of mischief rather than malice, but turned against the gods in the end. His three children with the giantess Angrboda were arch enemies of the gods – Fenrir, the dire wolf; Jormungand, the Midgard serpent; and Hel, ruler of the underworld.

After cutting off the golden hair of Thor's wife Sif, Loki went to the dwarfs to procure replacement hair. Betting his head that they could not do it, he challenged two dwarfs to compete in creating wonders for the gods, including Sif's golden hair, Odin's spear Gungnir and Thor's hammer. The gods judged the hammer the finest, but when the dwarfs asked for payment Loki refused. Unable to take off his head without also injuring his neck, the cheated dwarf sewed up Loki's lips with a leather thong.

The death of Balder

Balder, the son of Odin and Frigg, was called the Beautiful, and was beloved of all the gods; perhaps it was this that provoked the malice of the misfit Loki. Balder began to have troubled dreams, foreseeing his death, so Frigg asked everything in the world to promise not to harm her son. Everything did – fire, poison, disease, every animal and plant. So Balder was now safe.

The bored gods invented a game in which they encircled Balder and took turns throwing stones at him. Disguised as an old woman, Loki asked Frigg if everything in the world had promised never to harm Balder and she revealed that there was one sprig of mistletoe too young to swear the oath. Loki plucked this mistletoe, put it in the hand of Balder's blind brother, Hoder, and guided his throw. It struck Balder, who died. Their brother Hermod begged Hel to let Balder return to Asgard. She agreed, if every single thing in the world wept for his loss. Everything did, save for one giantess, Loki in disguise, who said, 'Let Hel keep him.' In revenge, the gods bound Loki to a stone until the end of the world.

Ragnarok

Ragnarok was an event yet to come, signalling the end of the world. The wolf Fenrir, the Midgard serpent Jormungand and their father Loki would break free of their bonds. The ship Naglfar, made from dead men's nails, would launch from Hel, with Loki as its steersman. The wolf would swallow the sun. From fiery Muspell, Surt would ride out with his sons, and Bifrost, the rainbow bridge, would shatter beneath them. Yggdrasil the world tree would shake with fear as the gods battled to the death with the hordes of Hel, the frost giants, and Surt and his sons. Thor would slay the Midgard serpent, before succumbing to its poison. Fenrir would swallow Odin. Then Surt would fling fire across the earth and burn up the whole world. After that, a new sun would be born, and a new earth would rise from the sea. Odin's sons Vidar and Vali would survive the battle, and settle where Asgard used to be, joined by Modi and Magni, the sons of Thor, and by Balder, released from Hel, with his blind brother Hoder. The world tree would shelter one man and one woman from the flames, Lif and Lifthrasir, who would feed on the morning dew, and beget a new human race.

Sigurd

Sigurd was a brave Norse youth favoured by the god Odin. He was raised by a smith called Regin, who forged the sword with which Sigurd killed the dragon Fafnir, Regin's transformed brother. Sigurd ate the dragon's heart; drenched by its blood, he became almost invulnerable. Sigurd took the dragon's treasure, which included a cursed ring.

Having drunk a potion that made him forget his true love – the Valkyrie Brynhild – Sigurd married Gudrun, daughter of the king of the Niflungs. When Gudrun's brother Gunnar wanted to marry Brynhild, Sigurd disguised himself as Gunnar, won Brynhild and gave her the fateful ring. Gudrun saw Brynhild wearing the ring and taunted her with the truth. Brynhild made brothers Gunnar and Högni kill Sigurd, then threw herself on Sigurd's funeral pyre. Gudrun married Brynhild's brother Atli, who killed Gunnar and Högni. So Gudrun murdered her own children by Atli, had their skulls made into cups and served Atli their blood as wine and their hearts as meat.

Sigurd the dragon slayer

Beowulf

The epic poem *Beowulf* is written in Old English, but concerns events that take place in Denmark and Sweden. Every night, the great hall of Hrothgar, king of the Danes, was visited by Grendel, a monster of the fens, who killed Hrothgar's men. Only Beowulf of the Geats tribe of Sweden was brave enough to swear to tackle the monster.

When the monster next attacked, Beowulf tore off its arm, and it fled screaming into the night, to die. The next night, after much feasting and rejoicing, the hall was besieged by Grendel's mother, intent on revenge. Beowulf tracked her to her watery lair and killed her with a great sword he found lying on the bottom of the lake. The waters boiled with blood and everyone assumed Beowulf was dead, but he emerged with the heads of Grendel and Grendel's mother. Beowulf went on to become a great king of the Geats, but fell in his old age when fighting a fire-breathing dragon that had been disturbed by someone stealing from its age-old treasure mound.

The Sutton Hoo helmet has dragon motifs, and also boar images like the helmets described in the Anglo-Saxon poem *Beowulf*.

The Sampo

The Finnish national epic, the *Kalevala*, was pieced together from orally transmitted poems by the 19th-century folklorist Elias Lönnrot. It centres on the first man, Väinämöinen, the son of Ilmatar, daughter of Air, who created the world. A singer and poet of magical powers, Väinämöinen found himself prisoner of his mortal enemy, the sorceress Louhi, in Northland. He gained his freedom – and her daughter, the Maid of the North – by promising Louhi a magical mill called the Sampo, which ground out corn, salt and money. Väinämöinen asked Ilmarinen, the smith who forged the sky, to make the mill for him in return for the maid. At first the maid refused to marry Ilmarinen, and when she did she soon died. When Ilmarinen's attempt to forge another wife from gold failed, Väinämöinen and he plotted to regain the Sampo. With the amorous adventurer Lemminkäinen, they sailed to the Northland and stole it. But Louhi sent storms to wreck their ship, and the Sampo was lost at sea. The parts that ground money and corn were broken, but it still grinds out salt to this day, which is why seawater is salty.

Karelian brothers Poavila and Triihvo Jamanen reciting Kalevala folk poems in 1894.

Myths of North America

A shared reverence for the earth and the sky, for the sacred power that is innate in the natural world, and for man's relationship with animals, unites the wide-ranging mythologies of North America's indigenous tribes. Many of the myths are set in the creation time, and tell of the First People, who were both human and animal. Often the world is made by dual creators, one high-minded and the other either cunning and mischievous like Coyote, or malicious like Flint, who mars every good gift of his twin brother in the mythology of the Seneca tribe.

The Ghost Dance movement of 1890 was supposed to bring about a renewal for Native Americans after centuries of hardship caused by white settlers. If they danced as the Paiute prophet Wovoka instructed them, a new world would roll in on a whirlwind, covering the old exhausted earth and sweeping the whites into the east; the dead would be reborn, and there would be a new age of peace and plenty. Such ideas have deep roots in Native American mythology, and still resonate today.

Nuxalk ceremonial mask representing the Moon (Tl'uk), with images of Whale and Raven.

Vacant, Empty and the Creation

In the beginning there was nothing at all, according to the Luiseño tribe of California. Two clouds formed in the empty space: one called Vacant and the other Empty. They were brother and sister. After trying many different forms, Empty said, 'I shall stretch myself out as big as I can. I shall shake and cause earthquakes. I shall roll around and around,' and she became the earth. Vacant said, 'I shall rise up high and arch over everything. I shall cause men to die and take their souls up to the world above,' and he became the sky. From this brother and sister everything that is to be found in this world was born.

Chingichnich succeeded these first deities. He instructed the people in their sacred ceremonies, taught them how to live and promised that, after death, they would live with him in the stars. He is still worshipped through the ritual drinking of *toloache*. Drunk by boys at their initiation into manhood, *toloache* induces visions through which the boys learn of the animal that is to be their sacred guide and helper through life.

The hallucinogenic *toloache* flower is still used in Luiseño initiation rituals.

Raven

According to the Tsimshian of the Northwest Coast, the first creator, Walks All Over the Sky, fell asleep, and the sparks that flew from his mouth became the stars. In the beginning, when stars were the only light, one of the animal-people lost a son and was sent a new child, called Raven, from the sky world.

At first Raven refused to eat, but then Mouth at Each End fed the child a scab from his shin bone, and Raven became so greedy that he ate all the food of the tribe. The chief sent him away, with berries and fish roe to scatter as he flew, to ensure he would never go hungry. Raven then flew up to the sky world and transformed into a leaf in a pool. When the sky chief's daughter drank from the pool, she swallowed the leaf and became pregnant with Raven. The new baby cried to play with the shiny light that hung in a box in the house. When he was given it, he put on his raven cloak and flew down to this world with the sun in a box. When he smashed the box, light spread through the sky.

Haida carving
of Raven

Turtle Island

The northeastern Seneca tell of a great tree in the centre of the sky. Ancient One pulled it up by the roots, leaving a hole, and pushed his wife Old Woman through it. This world was covered with water. The ducks wove their wings together to cushion Old Woman's fall and the Great Turtle rose from the depths to make a resting place for her. All the water creatures dived down to try to fetch soil to make her comfortable, but the water was too deep. The muskrat managed to smear some mud on his nose and when that was on the turtle's shell, it spread to create the earth. Old Woman had a daughter and this daughter was made pregnant by the wind, with two sons who argued in the womb. Flint was determined to be born first, and pushed his way out of his mother's armpit. She died giving birth to the second, Sky Holder. From her grave grew the three sisters who were the supporters of life – corn, beans and squash. Sky Holder and Flint created the world, but for every good thing Sky Holder made, Flint made something bad. So, for example, while Sky Holder made the first people out of clay, Flint introduced diseases to harm them.

World's Heart

For the Californian Achomawi, there was no land in the beginning, just water and darkness. There existed two gods: World's Heart and Annikadel, his grandson. World's Heart created the world and lives in its centre. Annikadel lives in the sky. His underparts are blue and white; as he travels through the sky the most anyone ever sees of him is a glint of light.

The First People, made by Annikadel from seeds and leaves, lived for thousands of years before humans arrived. They were animal-people. Annikadel sent a great flood, after which they were turned into animals or natural objects. Annikadel inspired one of these First People, Silkworm Man, to create the earth out of foam on the primal ocean. Other important First People were Coyote Man and Spider Woman. Coyote Man fixed north, west, south and east using four poles made from the rainbow. Spider Woman carried Annikadel in her cobweb basket up to separate the sun and the moon, and to fix the North Star and the South Star. Then World's Heart began turning the world over.

A contemporary
interpretation
of Coyote

Woge, the first people

The California Yurok believe the first race, the Real People, were *woge*, or 'first people' who 'instituted everything'. They formed the geography of the earth, and established laws of marriage and justice. Two heroes helped them – Wohpekumeu, who stole salmon and acorns for them, and laid down the laws of nature, and Pulekukwerek, who established the night sky and slew the primal monsters to make the world safe. Wohpekumeu was so potent with creation he needed only to look at a woman to make her pregnant; when he embraced the Skate woman, she would not let him go and carried him away across the ocean. Pulekukwerek also left, for a land where there is constant dancing.

Today's humans descend from the children of a dog woman. Once she began to have human children, her dog children were put out of the house; dogs now follow men, but men came from them. When humans came, the shy *woge* retreated, or transformed into animals, birds, rocks, landmarks and spirits. Today people still call on the *woge* in rituals, for they are still present in the world.

A Yurok cemetery

How Beaver brought the gift of fire

The Nez Perce of the Plateau talk of a time before people, when animals and trees moved about and talked, just as men do now. Only the pine trees had the gift of fire. No matter how cold it was, the pine trees huddled together around the warmth, and wouldn't share it.

One winter was so cold that everyone froze. Beaver swam up the Grande Ronde River to where the pine trees were warming themselves by a great fire. When a log rolled out from the fire and into the river, Beaver caught it, and swam away as fast as he could. The pines chased him, but they couldn't catch him, for he dodged from one side of the river to the other, which is why the river twists and turns. Most of the pines grew so tired they gave up, and they still stand by the side of the river today.

The last cedar could only watch as Beaver set fire to the willows, birches and other trees. Ever since that time, these trees have fire inside them that can be kindled using a fire drill.

How Coyote
freed the salmon

In the mythology of the Wishram Plateau tribe, the five Beaver sisters lived at Celilo Falls on the Columbia River and built a dam to trap salmon there. Coyote thought that the fish should be free for all. He transformed himself into a baby and floated down the river in a woven basket, crying 'Wah! Wah!' The five sisters rescued him and took him home.

Every day the sisters went to dig roots, leaving Coyote alone in the lodge. He made himself five wooden hats and five root-digging sticks. Then, day after day, while the sisters were out, Coyote put on his hats and undermined the dam using the root-digging sticks. By the time the sisters returned, he was back gurgling like a baby, but growing bigger every day. On the fifth day, the dam was nearly bursting, so Coyote didn't go back to the lodge. The sisters ran to the dam and hit him on the head with wooden clubs; each of their clubs broke on one of the five wooden hats. Coyote kept digging and, as the fifth hat broke, so did the dam. The salmon rushed upstream and now there was fish for everyone to eat.

Celilo Falls on the
Columbia River

The Ones Who Hold Our Roads

Early accounts of southwestern Zuni mythology speak of a creator, Awonawilona, who was both male and female, and was brought into being by the Earth Mother and Sky Father. But Awonawilona is better understood as a collection of powerful spirits rather than as a single being. These spirits, honoured in Zuni prayers and rituals, are known as the Ones Who Hold Our Roads. They include the Sun Father and Moonlight-Giving Mother.

The Sun Father had two houses, one in the eastern ocean and one in the western ocean. Moonlight-Giving Mother was his wife, but they were always separated. It was the Sun Father who brought the daylight people out of the underworld in order to give him offerings; in return he gave them blessings, including sunlight itself. According to the Zuni, the Ones Who Hold Our Roads were 'raw people', meaning they could transform themselves into any shape they wanted, unlike the daylight people who were 'cooked' in their human shape. Every person carries with them an invisible road that determines the length of their life.

Zuni kachina doll, representing one of the spirit beings impersonated by dancers in sacred ceremonies.

Wakonda

According to the Plains Omaha tribe, *Wakonda* is the power
that sustains the universe – not so much a god as an
unseen, all-pervading life force: the Great Mystery. *Wakonda*
is invisible and continuous, and manifests in two ways: first
by causing motion, for all movement of mind or body derives
from it and, second, by causing permanency of structure
and form, as in the landscape, the animals and man. *Wakonda*

The Sacred Pole

is perceived as being similar to will power. Through this mysterious power, all things are related to one another and to man – the seen to the unseen, the dead to the living, a fragment of anything to its entirety.

Wakonda sent the people a miraculous shining tree, from which was cut the sacred cottonwood pole known as the Venerable Man or the Sacred Pole. The Venerable Man has a basketwork of twigs filled with feathers around his middle and a scalp on the top of his head for hair. Returned to the Omaha Nation in 1989 after 100 years in a museum, the Sacred Pole contains the soul of the Omaha people.

Spider Woman

In southwestern Pueblo mythology, it was Thinking Woman who created the world from the web of her thoughts. When she took bodily form, it was as a spider, and as Spider Woman she was an important figure throughout the Southwest, with the power to give and take life. In Hopi myth, Spider Woman created the first people out of clay, making them in pairs: one male and one female.

One day, distracted, Spider Woman only made a man. Later she made a single woman, and sent her searching for the single man but, when they found each other, they argued all the time and eventually separated. This is the origin of all strife between husbands and wives.

Spider Woman taught the art of weaving and herself wove the moon from white cotton. When a Navajo woman uses Spider Woman's knowledge to weave a rug, she must weave a break into the pattern at the end, so that her soul may come back out to her and not be trapped in the web.

A Navajo woman weaving a rug

Daughter of the Sun

Elders of the southeastern Cherokee talk of the Sun, who lived at the far side of the sky, and her daughter, who lived in the middle. Every day, as she climbed along the sky arch, the Sun would stop at her daughter's house for her midday meal. The Sun was so strong no-one could look at her without screwing up their faces, but they smiled at the soft Moon.

The jealous Sun decided to kill all the people; she became ever hotter, so that many died. People turned into snakes to poison the Sun, but the Rattlesnake bit the Daughter of the Sun instead. When the Sun found her daughter dead, she shut herself in her house and would not come out. People stopped dying from the heat, but the whole world went dark and cold. Men tried to win Daughter of the Sun back from the Ghost Country, trapping her spirit in a box. But when they were nearly home they opened the box a crack, and her spirit flew out in the form of a red bird. The people sang songs to the Sun, and when they made her laugh she uncovered her face, and the world was filled with light once more.

Hiawatha

Sky Holder, the good creator, left this world to live in the sky, yet some say he chose to be born again as a mortal man, Hiawatha, 'he who makes rivers'. In those days all the nations were at war with each other. Among the Mohawk was a chief named Deganawida, who loved peace. But when he pleaded with the warriors to stop killing, they laughed at him. Sitting by a lake, he saw a man in a canoe lower a basket into the water, and bring it up again full of wampum shells, which he began to string. This was Hiawatha of the Onondaga. Deganawida asked him what he was doing, and Hiawatha explained that the wampum strings represented the rules of life, and were a symbol that peace should exist between the nations. They went to the Mohawk, the Oneida, the Cayuga and the Seneca, and all agreed to make peace and live by the new laws. But Atotarho of the Onondaga flew into a rage and his evil thoughts sprouted from his skull like serpents. Deganawida spoke gently to him, while Hiawatha combed the snakes from his hair, and Atotarho agreed to lead the five nations of the Iroquois League.

Flag of the Iroquois, based on a wampum-shell belt

Buffalo Woman
and Corn Woman

Buffalo Woman was a key figure in Plains mythology. She and Corn Woman were the source of the two main foods that sustained people. The Arikara tribe tell how Buffalo Woman travelled all over the world, searching for and summoning buffalo. Built with a post in each of the northeast, northwest, southwest and southeast corners, the Plains medicine lodge symbolizes the world and represents the four gods who hold up the heavens. The entrance to the lodge always faces east to allow the building to breathe as if it was human. Buffalo Woman's travels take place within the lodge. She walks from post to post, each time changing her moccasins, which completely wear out. 'Now I have gone all over the world,' she says.

The association between buffalo and corn is strong. One myth tells how a young man went hunting and saw a buffalo, standing on the first day looking east, then south, then west, then north, but he couldn't sneak up on it. On the fifth day, there was no buffalo, just the very first clump of corn.

Arikara girl

The Nightway ritual

The Nightway is one of many elaborate Navajo ceremonies of song, prayer, dance and ritual, known as 'chantways', which involve the creation and destruction of complex sand paintings. The Navajo name for these healing rituals means 'place where the gods come and go'. Each chantway has its own myths, and the Nightway has two alternative bodies of mythology: one called 'the Visionary' and one called 'the Stricken Twins'.

The first tells of a visionary named Bitahatini, who is taught the Nightway by the Holy People. The second tells of the twin sons of Talking God and a human girl. One is blind and the other lame, and they are cast out to wander the world. Talking God takes them to the Holy People, who institute the Nightway ritual as a cure. When they realize they are really being cured, the twins, who have been told to keep silent, call out with joy, and everything vanishes. Now they can only be cured if they pay. They cry and their crying turns into a song so plaintive the Holy People take pity on them and teach them the secrets and rituals of the Nightway.

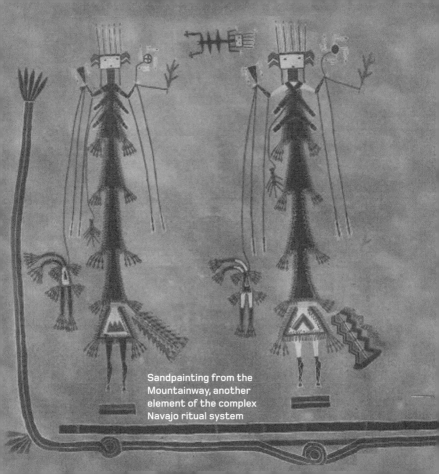

Sandpainting from the Mountainway, another element of the complex Navajo ritual system

The end of the world

According to the Pawnee nation of the Plains, the first race of humans was destroyed by a great flood. Tirawa, the creator, brought a new man and woman into being with the sound of his voice. He gave them the earth as their mother, and taught them how to build a timber lodge, and how to dance the Woman's Dance to call more buffalo from beneath the earth so the people would never starve.

Tirawa placed a great buffalo bull in the northwest to hold back the floodwaters. Every year this buffalo drops one hair, and when all the hairs have fallen off, the end will come for the current race. But Tirawa will not send another flood. Instead, the stars will sit in council and select a day when all things shall cease to be.

The command for the ending of all things will be given by the North Star and the South Star will carry out the commands. When the time comes, the Pawnee people will turn into stars and fly to the South Star.

Pawnee with a timber lodge

Sedna

While Moon Man is master of the land animals, Sea Woman, often called Sedna, is Mistress of the Sea Beasts. Sedna was originally human, but was persecuted – either because she married a dog or a sea bird, or simply because she was an unwanted orphan.

In a version told by the Netsilik of Canada, Sedna (known as Nuliajuk, the Ever-Copulating One) was pushed from an overloaded raft of kayaks. She tried to cling on, but her fingers were chopped off, and turned into the first seals. Sedna went to live in her house at the bottom of the sea. Whenever anyone broke a taboo, Sedna knew and shut up the sea beasts in the drip-basin beneath her lamp, so the people starved. A shaman had to make the terrifying journey to her house on the seabed, which was guarded by a fierce dog, and braid her hair for her. All the sins of humankind filter down through the sea and collect as dirt in Sedna's hair; she cannot brush it for herself with the stumps of her fingers.

Sculpture representing Sedna, goddess of the sea beasts.

The gift of joy

Once people knew no joy according to the myths of the Colville River Eskimo. All they did was work, eat and sleep. Every day was the same. There was a man and woman who had three sons, and lived by the sea. Every day the sons went hunting and brought their catch home to their parents. First the eldest son, and then the middle son, failed to return home. Now the family was dependent on the youngest son, Teriak. One day Teriak was stalking a caribou, when an eagle landed beside him and turned into a young man with a cloak of eagle feathers. The eagle asked Teriak the secret of life, and he answered that it was to work, eat and sleep. The eagle told Teriak that he had already killed his two brothers for giving this foolish answer. 'The secret of life is joy', he said. The eagle taught Teriak how to make a song and fit words to a tune, how to beat out a rhythm on a drum and how to dance. Then the eagle flew Teriak back home, and he and his parents held the first festival of song, attended by all the animal-people, to thank the eagles for their gift of joy.

Myths of Mexico and Central America

The mythologies of Mexico and Central America were shaped by Aztec and Maya culture. They are still alive today, in the myths of Nahuatl-speakers, such as the Sierra Nahuati, and Tzotzil-speakers, such as the Zinacantecs or the Chamulas. The myths of the ancient Zapotec and Mixtec cultures live on in today's peoples of Oaxaca. The Aztecs themselves inherited myths and gods from the earlier Toltecs, while both the Aztec and Maya cultures ultimately derive from that of the first major civilization in Guatemala and Mexico: the Olmecs.

Many shared elements, including blood sacrifice, the ritual ballgame, the feathered serpent and the Mesoamerican Long Count calendar, can be traced back to the Olmecs. Our knowledge of Aztec mythology is based both on pre-Hispanic screenfold codices and on the texts recorded by 16th-century friars, such as Bernardino de Sahagún. For the Maya, the most important sources are the Popol Vuh, which tells the story of the hero twins Xbalanque and Hunahpu, and the various Books of Chilam Balam.

Mayan pyramid at Chichen Itza

The Aztec Creation

The Aztecs conceived of the world as being made, destroyed and re-created in a series of 'suns'. The gods persisted through these suns. Most of the work of creation and destruction fell to two brothers: Quetzalcoatl and Tezcatlipoca. These two gods were sometimes allies, sometimes adversaries. Together, they made the earth and sky of the present world – the world of the fifth sun – by slaying the earth monster Tlaltecuhtli.

Quetzalcoatl and Tezcatlipoca saw Tlaltecuhtli striding over the sea, ravenous for flesh. Her mouth was full of flint blades and she also sprouted mouths from her elbows and knees. The two gods transformed themselves into serpents. One seized the left hand and right foot of Tlaltecuhtli, the other the right hand and left foot. Then the gods tore Tlaltecuhtli in two, throwing one half into the sky and creating the earth with the other half. From her hair came the trees and flowers, from her eyes, wells and springs, from her mouth, rivers, from her nose, mountains. Tlaltecuhtli can be heard crying out in the night for the hearts of men to eat.

Tlaltecuhtli

Quetzalcoatl,
the plumed serpent

Quetzalcoatl was half rattlesnake, half quetzal bird, although he was often depicted in human form. As Ehecatl, he was the god of wind, described as the roadsweeper of the life-giving rain gods. The sun only moved because it was blown by his breath.

Once Quetzalcoatl and Tezcatlipoca had remade the world of the fifth sun, Quetzalcoatl descended to Mictlan, the underworld, to retrieve the bones of a previous race. He asked the skeletal god of death Mictlantecuhtli for the bones. Mictlantecuhtli agreed, on condition that Quetzalcoatl travelled four times around his realm sounding a conch trumpet, but gave him a conch with no holes. Quetzalcoatl called for worms to drill holes and bees to enter the conch and magnify its sound. As Quetzalcoatl left with the bones, Mictlantecuhtli caused him to fall into a deep pit. The bones were nibbled and broken by a quail – that's why people are all different sizes. Quetzalcoatl gathered the bones and had them ground into flour by the goddess Cihuacoatl. Then the gods shed blood onto the flour and from this mixture a new race of humans was made.

Tezcatlipoca,
the smoking mirror

Tezcatlipoca was the god of rulers, sorcerers and warriors. Aztec accounts of the five worlds, or suns, show a constant rivalry between Tezcatlipoca and his brother Quetzalcoatl. In the mythical histories of the Aztecs, Quetzalcoatl is described as the king of the Aztec city of Tollan and Tezcatlipoca as his treacherous brother and sorcerer.

Quetzalcoatl is credited with having introduced the Aztec calendar, and as having taught humankind many arts and sciences. Falling out with his brother over the issue of human sacrifice, Quetzalcoatl shut himself in the house of prayer and shed his own blood to the gods in auto-sacrifice. He became terrible to look at, wasting away so that his eyeballs bulged. Scheming Tezcatlipoca sent him a mirror so that he could see how terrible he looked. Then Tezcatlipoca tricked him into getting drunk and sleeping with his sister Quetzalpetlatl. Quetzalcoatl was so ashamed he sailed away on a raft of serpents. When Hernàn Cortès landed in 1519, the Aztecs believed him to be Quetzalcoatl returned.

Creation of the fifth sun

After the creation of the new earth and sky from the body of the earth monster Tlaltecuhtli, the gods gathered at Teotihuacan, the place where time began, to decide who should become the new sun to light up the world. A proud god named Tecuciztecatl volunteered, and the gods also chose the humble and diseased god Nanahuatzin. Two hills known as the Pyramids of the Sun and Moon were made for these gods, where they could fast and do penance before casting themselves into a sacrificial pyre. Tecuciztecatl made the finest offerings, while those of Nanahuatzin were simple – maguey spines spotted with his own blood, and scabs from his body as incense. After four days the gods called for the pair to enter the blazing pyre. Tecuciztecatl ran up, but was driven back by the flames. Nanahuatzin cast himself into the heart of the fire and was consumed; Tecuciztecatl followed. The gods turned their eyes to the sky to see Nanahuatzin reappear in glory as the sun and Tecuciztecatl nearly as bright as the moon. The gods threw a rabbit into the face of the moon to dim it.

An Aztec stone calendar with the fifth sun at its centre.

Aztec sacrifices
to the gods

The Aztecs felt they owed a blood debt to the gods, who had sacrificed their own blood in the making of humanity and had offered their hearts to set the fifth sun in motion. They let their own blood, typically from tongue, ear lobe or penis, in acts of auto-sacrifice. Aztecs also offered a regular sacrifice of still-beating human hearts to the sun god Huitzilopochtli. They practised a kind of warfare known as 'flowery war', in which they captured as many of the enemy as possible. The Aztecs cut the hearts from their victims using obsidian blades, and offered them to the gods in a vessel known as an eagle gourd. The victims were then flayed and decapitated, and their skulls exhibited in a rack.

The ritual year called for many sacrifices. Every 260 days a man representing the underworld god Mictlantecuhtli was sacrificed at night in the temple of Tlaxiacco, and his blood mixed with dough to be eaten by the celebrants, who thus communed with the gods. Not all sacrifice was gruesome: the gods appreciated smoke from incense and tobacco, as well as gifts of food and precious objects.

The Maya Creation

In the beginning there was nothing but sea and sky. Coiled in the sea was the plumed serpent Gucumatz. Hovering in the sky was Heart of Sky. The two began to discuss what to create; as they spoke their words summoned mountains and earth from the waters, and filled them with trees, animals and birds.

When the creators asked the animals to worship them, they just squawked and howled. The gods tried again, making a man out of clay, but he was too weak and crumbly and dissolved before their eyes. They consulted the diviners Xpiyacoc and Xmucane, who told them people should be made of wood. So they made a new race, fashioning the men from wood and the women from rushes, but these people had no souls and refused to worship their creators; Gucumatz and Heart of Sky drowned them in a flood. At this time there was no sun, but a great macaw with metal eyes and precious stones for teeth called Vucub Caquix set himself up as a false sun; he was shot with blowguns by the Hero Twins (see page 264), so the true sun could rise.

Bust of the plumed
serpent Gucumatz

Hun Hunahpu,
the god of maize

The Maya Hun Hunahpu (One Blowgunner) was the father of the Hero Twins Xbalanque and Hunahpu, and also of the monkey twins Hun Batz and Hun Chuen, the patron gods of writing, art and calculation. Hun Hunahpu was the god of maize, depicted as a beautiful young man with a flat, elongated forehead and a shaved head with just a tuft of hair imitating an ear of corn.

When maize was harvested, the action mimicked the decapitation of Hun Hunahpu by the death gods of Xibalba, the underworld (see page 264). The first maize was fetched for the creators Gucumatz and Heart of Sky by the fox, coyote, parrot and crow, and was ground into meal by Hun Hunahpu's mother Xmucane. From this meal the first four men were made. They were very intelligent and could see all over the world. Although these men worshipped their creators, Heart of Sky thought they were too perfect, so blurred their vision so that they could only see near things and understand only so much. Then four women were made, to be their companions.

Mayan stela showing the king 18 Rabbit in the role of the maize god as he danced at creation.

The Hero Twins

Hun Hunahpu and Vucub Hunahpu were Maya twins whose noisy ballgame riled the death gods. Luring the twins down to Xibalba, the death gods killed them and put Hun Hunahpu's head in a tree. The head impregnated the maiden Xquic with its spittle, and she gave birth to the Hero Twins, Hunahpu and Xbalanque.

The death gods challenged the Hero Twins to a ritual ballgame. The twins won, but were thrown into the House of Lances. They escaped, only to be imprisoned in the Houses of Cold, Jaguars, Fire and Bats. Boasting that they were immortal, the twins had themselves sacrificed and their bones ground into flour, then came back to life. The death gods were so impressed they demanded the same be done to them. The Hero Twins killed the lords of death, but did not revive them. The twins then ascended to the sky, where they became the sun and moon. The sacred ballgame was played all over Central America and pre-Hispanic Mexico; it was connected to ideas about human sacrifice, which was required by the gods in return for the gift of fire.

Yajval Balamil, the Zinacantec earth lord

The Tzotzil-speaking Zinacantec people are modern descendants of the Maya. A veneer of Catholicism overlays a deep relation to their Maya heritage. Crosses by caves and waterholes all over Zinacantán are regarded as channels of communication with Yajval Balamil, the earth owner, a powerful god who must be placated before any work is done on the land.

If a man enters one of Yajval Balamil's caves, he may be rewarded with money or livestock, or he may be pressed into servitude to look after Yajval Balamil's herds of mules. One man was given only a pair of iron sandals and told he must work for the earth lord until they were worn out. He worked as a muleteer under the earth until the sandals were worn out, then went home to his disbelieving wife – until eight mule loads of money arrived, his pay from Yajval Balamil. The *kalvarios* or cross shrines of Zinacantán are meeting places of the ancestral gods. Maize plants, the most important crop, are called 'the sunbeams of the gods', and believed to have an inner soul, just like humans.

Deliberately broken Maya pottery found in caves may be a ritual offering to Yajval Balamil.

Myths of South America

Inca mythology splits between a state mythology that glorifies Inti, the sun god, and establishes the Inca emperors as his heirs, and the myths of the Hatunruna, the common people. The myths of the latter were more local and particular to their interests; their descendants are the modern-day Quechua and Aymara. The Hatunruna worshipped the mummified bodies of their ancestors and believed that the landscape inherited from them was alive with the spirits of the *huacas* (sacred places). This kind of belief, focused on the *ayllu*, an extended family group attached to a particular territory, reaches both forward to today and backwards to the beginning of Andean culture in prehistory. The formalized mythology that underpinned Inca power is unlike the local tribal mythologies found elsewhere in South America. All across the continent – from the Orinoco delta in the north to Tierra del Fuego in the far south – there are scores of South American Indian cultures, each with its own distinct and rich mythology. Much of this great inheritance of myth concerns the animal-people ancestors of the creation time.

Inca ruins at
Machu Picchu

Inti, the Inca sun god

In the Temple of the Sun in Cuzco there was a golden image of the sun god Inti, showing him as a human face surrounded by golden rays. The worship of Inti was a specifically Inca, rather than a pan-Andean cult and the Inca emperors believed that, as direct descendants of the sun god, they ruled by divine right.

The emperor was the son of the sun, the Incas were the children of the sun and gold was the sweat of the sun. The first Inca emperor, Manco Capac, emerged at the Island of the Sun on Lake Titicaca, and regarded himself as the true son of the sun. Some accounts say he dazzled the people of the Cuzco valley by standing on a hill at dawn in two plates of gold, to fool them by imitating the sun.

The Incas believed that the sun and the stars were at war, and tried to tie them together by rituals at the Hitching-Post of the Sun at Machu Picchu. They pleaded with the creator god Viracocha, 'May the world not turn over.'

Viracocha,
the Inca creator

Viracocha was the creator of earth and time, having emerged in the primal darkness at Lake Titicaca. First he made a race of giants, but they angered him so he drowned them and turned them to stone. Then Viracocha summoned the sun, the moon and the stars from the Island of the Sun in the centre of the lake.

From still malleable stones by the lakeside, Viracocha shaped the first men and women, painting them with clothes, and giving each group its own language, songs and seeds to plant for food. At the same time he created all the animals and birds, making a male and female of each, and giving each bird its distinctive song. Then he sent the people underground, each group to emerge from caves at the places where they were to live. He kept two people with him: Imaymana Viracocha and Tocapo Viracocha, said to be his sons. Viracocha and his sons travelled through the land, calling for the people to emerge from underground and teaching them how to live. When they reached the coast of Ecuador they carried on walking across the waves into the west.

Coniraya Viracocha, the Andean creator

The foundation myths of the common people, the Hatunruna, are very different to those of the ruling Inca. For the Hatunruna, the whole landscape was alive with *huacas*, or sacred places, which could be personified. The Hatunruna told tales of a trickster god known as Coniraya Viracocha, who made the villages, the fields and the irrigation channels.

Coniraya Viracocha travelled the earth disguised as a poor Indian. He attempted to seduce Cavillaca, a virgin *huaca*, but she rejected him. Coniraya spilled his semen into a fruit; eating it, Cavillaca fell pregnant. A year later, Cavillaca summoned all the male gods who arrived dressed in finery except for Coniraya in his rags. Her baby climbed into Coniraya's lap and Cavillaca was so dismayed, she fled. Coniraya pursued her. On the way he met all the animals, naming them and giving them good or bad characteristics according to how helpful they were. When Coniraya caught up with Cavillaca and her son, he found them turned to rocks in the sea. They still lie there, by the ruins of the temple of Pachacamac, the coastal god.

The famous Nazca lines depict Andean animals and mythical symbols.

Pachacamac

Pachacamac was the creator god whose pilgrimage site was on the central coast of Peru, just south of Lima. One myth calls him 'the son of the sun'. At the beginning of time, Pachacamac created the first man and woman, but did not provide them with food, so the man soon died. The woman begged the sun for help and he made her pregnant with his rays. After just four days she gave birth to a boy. Pachacamac resented this; he killed and dismembered the boy, and planted his body.

From the boy's teeth sprang corn, from his ribs and bones, yucca, and from his flesh all manner of vegetables and fruits. The sun took the boy's penis and navel and used them to make a new child, named Vichama, who went travelling. Pachacamac killed the woman he had made and fed her to the vultures. He then made a new human couple who began to populate the land. On his return, Vichama resurrected his mother, and turned the people made by Pachacamac into stone and, later, *huacas*, or sacred places. Then Vichama asked the sun to create a new race of humanity.

Sacred places like this *huaca* are the remains of Pachacamac's second human race.

Dauarani,
the Mother of the Forest

Warao means 'boat people', and the Warao people virtually live in their *cachicamo* (tree canoes). A Warao boat-maker is called to the craft in a dream that binds him to the service of Dauarani, who was born from the first canoe. To reach the radiant box-like house of Dauarani, the boat-maker must travel through the body of a rainbow serpent, holding the secret of boat-making in his hands. The building of each boat recreates his initial vision in a mystical search for spiritual bliss. Each boat is a lovingly crafted image of Dauarani.

The first dugout canoe was made by Haburi. When Haburi was a baby, his father Roaster was killed by an evil spirit, which chased his two wives and Haburi to the house of the frog-woman, Wauta. She magically stretched Haburi into a grown boy and he committed incest with his mothers. When they realized the truth, Haburi invented the canoe so they could escape from the frog-woman. When no longer needed, the canoe turned into Dauarani, who is called the Mother of the Forest.

The origin of death

In the beginning, according to the myths of the Caduveo of Brazil, people who died revived two days later, as if waking from sleep. Caracara, the hawk and trickster companion of the creator Gô-noêno-hôdi, did not like this awakening of the dead. He said to Gô-noêno-hôdi, 'Whoever dies must really die. The world is already so full of people, soon there will be no more room.' Gô-noêno-hôdi agreed and did as Caracara suggested.

But when Caracara's mother died, Caracara went weeping to Gô-noêno-hôdi, begging for his mother to be revived. Gô-noêno-hôdi told him to pick one of the red lilies that grew in the marshes, to go to her grave, to get her to hold the stem and to pull her back out into life. Caracara did as he had been told and his mother began to come back into life. Caracara could already see her face when the fragile stem broke, and his mother fell back into death. Caracara went back to Gô-noêno-hôdi, weeping and begging, but Gô-noêno-hôdi told him, 'There's no help for it now, Caracara. Your mother must stay dead.'

The caracara falcon is widespread across south and central America.

Lem, the Sun Man

The first sun, Táruwalem, was cruel. In the myths of the Yamana of Chile and Argentina, when he was angry he grew so hot he would boil the ocean and burn the forest. In those days the women ruled, led by Hánuxa the moon-woman, and they decided to kill Táruwalem. They almost strangled him to death, but he fled into the sky, much weakened, and became a star. Táruwalem's son, Lem, the Sun Man, was kind and good, and a great hunter. One day while hunting he stumbled across the secrets of the women's sacred *kina*-hut, and heard the women practising to imitate the spirits. He told the men and they rose up against the rule of the women. In a great battle, all the women were killed or transformed into the animals of land and sea, except for Hánuxa. She went up to the sky with her husband Akáinix, the rainbow, and Lem, the Sun Man. After that time, it was the men who gathered in the *kina*-hut. The scars of battle can still be seen on the face of Hánuxa, the moon; she was so angry afterwards that she plunged into the sea and caused a world flood that destroyed all the animal-people, save for a few who took refuge on the mountaintops.

Yamana ceremonial *kina*-hut in Tierra del Fuego

Myths of Africa

Myths have been told in Africa for thousands of years, in more than a thousand languages. They remain an integral part of the mental and spiritual landscape of many African cultures, reflecting a supernatural dimension filled with gods and spirits that overlaps the visible world. Although there are borrowings from, and echoes in, related cultures, there is no sense in which one could construct a meaningful pan-African mythology. The nature and concerns of the myths vary wildly. For example, the myths of the Shilluk of the Upper Nile focus narrowly on the foundation and organization of Shilluk society and its system of divine kingship; whereas, the myths of the Dogon of Mali concentrate in such fine and subtle detail on creation and the great cosmic themes that they are almost too complex for any outsider to grasp. Myths of West Africa were taken to the New World by slaves. In Haiti, the gods of the Fon, Arada, Nago, Congo, Ibo, Bomba, Limba and Bambara mingled with those of the Carib Indians to produce voodoo.

The Dogon cosmos

The Dogon people of Mali, western Africa, have one of the most intricate mythological systems ever recorded. Every single aspect of Dogon life is imbued with myth.

The whole universe was originally contained in an egg or seed, and everything that exists began as a spiral vibration inside this egg – a helical expansion of the universe that still continues today. Everything, from the smallest seed to the expanse of the cosmos, reflects and expresses all things. A village, or a homestead, or a hat or a fruit – all of these things can contain the whole universe.

Each Dogon village is regarded as a living person. It lies north to south with the smithy at its head and shrines at its feet, because the creator Amma made the world from clay in the form of a woman lying in this position. The hut of the *hogon*, or headman, is a model of the cosmos, and his movements within it are attuned to the rhythms of the universe. His pouch is the 'pouch of the world'; his staff is 'the axis of the world'.

The head of a Dogon
medicine staff

Nyikang

Nyikang is the mythical personification of kingship for the Shilluk of the Upper Nile, a being who can bring wind and rain. Nyikang led the Shilluk to their present homeland and his spirit lives in every king. Nyikang is also the bridge between man and the remote creator of the world, Juok. Nyikang refused to swear allegiance to his half-brother Duwat. As Nyikang left, Duwat gave him a stick for planting sorghum, saying it should be used to dig the ground of his new village. Nyikang led his people to a river, where they settled. Nyikang's cow ran away to the kingdom of the sun and Ojul, the grey hawk, went to look for her. Garo, the son of the sun, denied the cow was there, but Ojul returned to Nyikang and told him the cow was in the herd of a tall man wearing a silver bracelet – Garo. Nyikang gathered his army, but when they came to the sun the army was destroyed. Nyikang cut off Garo's hand and seized the bracelet. He threw an adze at the sun. When he touched his dead army with the silver bracelet, the men came back to life. Nyikang did not die, but disappeared in a whirlwind.

Two Shilluk
warriors

The rainbow serpent

For the Fon of West Africa, Aido-Hwedo, the cosmic serpent, has twin male and female forms: one in the sea and one in the sky. Aido-Hwedo carried the creator, Mawu-Lisa (also both female and male), in its mouth as the world was made, and that is why the world curves and winds. When all the work was done, Mawu-Lisa saw that there was too much weight for the calabash-shaped earth to bear, so asked Aido-Hwedo to curl around beneath it like a carrying pad. Mawu-Lisa created the cool sea for Aido-Hwedo to lie in.

There are 3,500 serpent coils above the earth and 3,500 below. Aido-Hwedo eats iron bars that are forged for him by red monkeys that live beneath the sea; when the supply of iron runs out, the starving Aido-Hwedo will gnaw his own tail and the world with all its burdens will tip into the sea. Aido-Hwedo represents the creative power and living quality of everything that is flexible, sinuous and moist, such as the rainbow, the tides, smoke and even the nerves.

A Fon representation of
the serpent chewing his
tail from Benin

Ifa divination

Ifa is the god of fate. Ifa divination, practised in many parts of West Africa and also in the New World, is regarded as 'the cornerstone of Yoruba culture'. Ifa priests are consulted at every important juncture in life. They seek to petition and appease the *orisha*, or benevolent gods, such as Shango, god of thunder, and Ogun, god of iron and war, and the *ajogun*, or malevolent gods, such as Iku, god of death, and Arun, god of disease.

Crucial to this balance is the trickster god Eshu, who is messenger and mediator between gods and men. Eshu holds the balance in the cosmic struggle between the two groups of gods. But Eshu can only help those who sacrifice to him, in a ritual presided over by a priest wearing a statuette of the two-faced god hooked over his shoulder. Eshu can then present this sacrifice to the relevant *ajogun*. Before birth, each human being selects his or her *ori,* or spiritual head; a person who selects a defective *ori* has to make ceaseless sacrifice in order to progress in life.

The trickster god Eshu is a many-sided character who can assume 256 different forms.

Anansi and the sky god

Kwaku Anansi, the spider trickster of Asante myth, makes fools of men and gods alike. Once he went up to the sky god Onyankopon and asked if he could buy the stories for which the god was famous. Onyankopon, who had refused his stories to many rich and powerful kings, specified a price he thought unpayable: Anansi was to bring him Onini the python, Osebo the leopard, Mmoboro the swarm of hornets and Mmoatia the forest spirit. Anansi told him he would bring them and he would add his old mother Nsia, too. Anansi consulted his wife Aso, and she helped him. He tricked Onini into measuring himself against a palm branch and tied him to it with creeper. He tricked Osebo by trapping him in a pit. He tricked Mmoboro by fooling the swarm into thinking it was raining, so luring them into a gourd. He tricked Mmoatia by making a doll sticky with tree sap, which Mmoatia stuck to when she slapped it. Anansi took them to Onyankopon, along with his old mother, and Onyankopon gave him the stories with his blessing. Now they are called spider, or Anansi, stories.

The rain queue

The Lovedu or Lobedu of the Transvaal, in South Africa, are ruled by a rain queen, Mujaji (or Modjadji). She is the transformer of the clouds and even her emotions affect the rain. She not only brings the rain, but also orders the seasons. A rain queen dies by ritual suicide and not of natural causes. After her death comes drought and famine.

The rain charms and sacred beads of the rain queen were stolen for her by the mother of the mythical founder of the Lovedu, Dzugudini. Dzugudini was the daughter of a sacred king who committed incest with her brother. When she would not reveal who was the father of her son Makaphimo, she had to flee her father's wrath. Dzugudini is now among the ancestors who must be honoured if the queen is to make rain, for if the ancestors are displeased, they may prevent her doing so by 'holding the queen's hands'. The most important religious ceremony of the Lovedu year is the annual offering of beer to the ancestors in thanksgiving for the harvest.

A masked dancer undergoes the Lovedu *vuwhera* initiation from boyhood to manhood.

/Kaggen and the eland

The San creator /Kaggen (the backslash denotes a clicking sound) is a trickster who created the world by dreaming it into being. Envisaged as a man, he can take any form, his favourites being the mantis and the eland antelope. /Kaggen particularly loved elands, and tried to protect them from hunters; only the elands ever knew where he was.

/Kaggen created the first eland from a piece of the shoe of his son-in-law, Kwammang-a, the rainbow. At first the creature was only small, but /Kaggen called it to come to him, and rubbed it with honeycomb to make it shine and fed it honey to make it grow. Kwammang-a and his son /Ni-opwa, the ichneumon wasp, spied on /Kaggen and the eland. Kwammang-a waited for it to come and drink at the pool and killed it. When /Kaggen saw Kwammang-a cutting up the eland, he wept. /Kaggen took the eland's gall bladder and pierced it with a stick. Darkness poured out and engulfed the world. So that there should be some light, /Kaggen threw his own shoe into the sky, where it became the moon.

San rock paintings depict hunting
scenes of elands and other animals.

The San origin of death

The moon, formed from the shoe of the creator /Kaggen, walks across the night sky. When he is full, the sun pierces him with a knife, and then he decays until only his backbone is left. Then, according to /Kaggen's promise, the moon is slowly reborn, gaining life and vigour as he waxes.

Originally the moon intended for people to be reborn too, but one of the animal-people of the creation time, a hare, caused death to come into the world. The hare was weeping for his dead mother, crying that she was dead and would never come back. The moon comforted him, saying that his mother was only sleeping and that she would come back, but the hare would not listen to him.

Eventually the moon became so angry he struck the hare on the mouth, leaving a scar on his lip that is still there today. The moon cursed the hare, saying, 'As for men, now they shall die and never return'.

African gods in
the New World

Voodoo, in its various forms, is a religion without any formal structure. It is essentially a religion of divine possession, in which ecstatic dancers circle a post that links earth and heaven, and are 'ridden' by the spirits of the *Iwa* (gods).

Many of the 12 million Africans transported to the Caribbean and North America as slaves were Fon, Yoruba and Ewe tribespeople from West Africa. They took their gods with them into exile, where the various myths and rituals fused into a new religion. In North America and Haiti this religion is called voodoo or vodou; in Brazil, *candomblé*; in Cuba, *santería*; in Jamaica, *obeayisne*; and in Trinidad, *shango* cult. The word 'voodoo' derives from the Fon *vodun*, meaning gods or spirits. The voodoo religions took shape under the cover of Christianity. Each of the voodoo gods or *iwa* is identified with a Catholic saint. Thus Legba, the keeper of the crossroads between the human and supernatural worlds, is identified with Sts Peter and Andrew; Gédé, the *iwa* of the dead, with St Expedit; and Ezili, the *iwa* of love, with the Virgin Mary.

Religious symbol of Papa Legba, used in voodoo rituals.

Myths of Oceania

The extraordinarily rich mythologies of Oceania can be divided into four main categories. Polynesian myth, especially in New Zealand and Hawaii, is the most structured, with a pantheon of gods and an interconnection between myth and social structure. In Micronesia, myths on coral atolls, such as Ifaluk, reveal a poetic and peaceful world in which cultural achievements such as navigation or body art, are celebrated. In Melanesia, myths in New Guinea or the Torres Straits reflect a mythology that is 'embedded' in the landscape and also the importance of creation-time ancestors.

This notion of embedded myth is key to understanding the mythology of the Australian Aborigines, for whom 'country' is the central concept that validates and sustains culture. Aborigines conceive of Australia, but most especially their own 'country' (which includes people, plants, and animals as well as landscape), as a kind of living myth. Every hill, rock, creek or waterhole reveals the tracks of the ancestral beings of the Dreaming, alive with limitless potential for restoration and renewal.

The mysterious giant heads of Easter Island are known as *moai*, and represent the spiritual power of great chiefs.

Tangaroa gives birth to the gods

In New Zealand, Tangaroa is the god of the sea, and all gods, including Tangaroa, are the offspring of Rangi, the sky, and Papa, the earth. But on a number of Polynesian islands, Tangaroa (or A'a) is the creator of all things.

In the beginning, Tangaroa was alone in the darkness, inside a shell. Nothing else existed. At last Tangaroa broke the shell, calling out, 'Who's there?' But there was no one. Tangaroa used the top half of the shell to make the sky, and the bottom half to make the rock and sand. He then used his own body to complete the creation, making a mountain range from his backbone, the earth from his flesh, and using his fingernails and toenails to make the scales and shells of fish.

Tangaroa then called the other gods out from within himself. With the help of the craftsman god Tu, he created men and women. Echoing this myth, everything in the world is a kind of shell – the sky, the earth, a woman's womb.

A wooden carving featuring the ancestral figure known as Tangaroa

Tane and Hine-titama

The Maori god of the forest, Tane, desired a partner, so he mixed mud and sand and shaped it into a woman, Hine-hau-one, the Earth-formed Maiden. She bore him a daughter, Hine-titama, the Dawn Maiden. Hine-titama, too, became Tane's wife.

One day, when Tane was absent looking for beautiful objects to ornament the world, Hine-titame went down to the village and innocently asked who her father was. When she heard the answer, she fled to the dark underworld, Po. Tane tried to follow her, but the underworld was closed to him. Hine-titama told him to stay in the light and nurture their offspring, while she would stay in the darkness and drag their offspring down. She was no longer the Dawn Maiden, but Hine-nui-te-po, the Great Goddess of Darkness, who sucks all living things down to their death.

The only thing that does not die is the moon. When it wanes, the moon goes to bathe in the living waters of Tane and is restored in strength, to travel once more across the sky.

Carving of Tane

Maui of a thousand tricks

Maui, the Polynesian trickster was born as a foetus, his mother Hina having got pregnant by putting on a man's loincloth. Hina gave Maui a magic fishhook that once belonged to Kuula, the god of fishing. Maui caught a fish so huge that he could not pull it clear of the sea — he had fished up the islands of Polynesia.

Thinking that the days were too short, Maui tried to lasso the sun with a rope of coconut fibre, but the sun burned through it. So he made a rope of his sister's hair and snared the sun as it rose. Maui refused to free the sun until it agreed to shine longer in the summer and to move quickly through the sky in the winter.

Maui wished to conquer death and descended to the underworld to rape the Great Goddess of Darkness Hine-nui-te-po. He crawled inside her, meaning to emerge from her mouth, but when his little legs were waving outside her, the birds began to laugh and woke the sleeping goddess, who crushed Maui to death between her thighs.

Makemake
and the Bird Man

To help them remember their long sacred chants, the priests of Rapa Nui carved hieroglyphs on wooden boards called *rongorongo*. Most of these seem to involve creation myths, recording the familiar Polynesian pattern of an evolving creation starting from the union of light and dark, and propelled by a chain of procreation. One line of such a chant from Rapa Nui tells us that 'Small Thing by lying with Imperceptible Thing made the Fine Dust in the Air'.

The goggle-eyed, skull-faced, bird god Makemake is credited with creating humans by masturbating into clay. He and his wife Haua first drove the seabirds across the sea to Rapa Nui, settling them on the rocks at Orongo. Every July brave swimmers competed to find the first egg, the winner becoming the sacred Bird Man, Makemake's representative on earth, for the coming year. The egg was believed to generate food. In a wooden image of Makemake, the god is shown as half starved – a reminder of the islanders' constant struggle to feed themselves in this remote place.

Hieroglyphs on a wooden rongorongo board

The Work of the Gods

Every aspect of Tikopia life was governed by a complex ritual cycle known as the Work of the Gods, which has affinities with other Polynesian ritual systems, such as the Makahiki of Hawaii or the Inasi of Tonga.

The Work of the Gods was divided into two six-week ritual cycles: the Work of the Trade Wind and the Work of the Monsoon. Major rites included the re-dedication of the sacred canoes; the re-consecration of the temples; harvest and planting rites; and the manufacture of turmeric, which was used as a ritual body paint and as a sacred dye. The purpose was to maintain contact with the *atua*, powerful spiritual beings whose favour was required to feed the Tikopia and guard their health.

These gods and spirits were appeased with food and kava, and asked with elaborate formality to ensure plentiful harvests of crops, such as breadfruit or yams.

The intoxicating drink kava is made by pounding the roots of the kava plant and adding the pulp to water.

The origin of tattooing

On the coral atoll of Ifaluk, the traditional tattoos that women admire on their lovers are said to have originated with the trickster god Wolfat who, being a god, could 'put on' tattoos and then take them off again. He lived in the sky of flowers with the other gods. His father Lugweilang visited all the islands every day and reported back to the sky god Aluelap on how the people were faring.

One day Wolfat looked down from the sky and saw a beautiful woman and decided to visit her that night. The woman awoke to find a strange man in her house and lit a fire so she could see who it was. When she saw the black tattoos all over Wolfat's body, she was overcome with desire. In the morning Wolfat returned to the sky of flowers. When he came back that night, he was undecorated. The woman rejected him, only allowing him into her bed when he had put the tattoos back on. The next day Wolfat showed the Ifaluk men how to tattoo themselves, using black soot and a bird's wing.

Geb, the sun god

Geb, sun god of the Marind-Anim of New Guinea, is said to be the son of Nubog and Dinadin, the earth and the sky, but it is also said that he originated from himself; 'growing he did grow'.

Geb was a red-skinned man who lived in an anthill that radiated unbearable heat. Because of this, no woman would marry him – he had to make do with a piece of bamboo stem. Geb would kidnap human children, take them back to his fiery lair and cut off their heads. Urged on by their womenfolk, the fearful men poured water onto the anthill to quench the heat and, when Geb emerged, they cut off his head. Frightened by this assault, Geb's head fled eastwards, underground, to Kondo, the place of the sunrise. There, the head climbed up a yam tendril into the sky, to become the sun.

Every day Geb travels from Kondo to the western horizon, then back underground to Kondo through the night, to rise again the following morning.

The Dreaming

The concept of the Dreaming is central to the spiritual and intellectual life of Australian Aborigines. It used to be known as the Dreamtime, but is a continuous and ongoing process, rather than something that happened in the remote past.

The Dreaming is the real, eternal present, accessible through ritual, sacred objects, song, dance, storytelling and visual art. The whole landscape of Australia is alive with the eternal potency of the Dreaming. Myths tell of the wanderings across the land of the 'First People' in a time when the world was still plastic, malleable and in a state of creation. These ancestral beings were asleep in the primal world. When they woke they shaped human beings and a landscape in which they could live; then they transformed themselves into geographical features. Dreamings are always intimately tied in with the landscape – placed within it. The actions of the First People infused the land with their spiritual essence, their *djang*, and it is this that makes the land alive.

Aboriginal rock art with open-hand stencils, one of the most ancient symbols of humankind.

Lumaluma

Lumaluma was a whale who came out of the sea and took the form of a man. He stole two wives while their husbands were fishing, and travelled west with them, bringing sacred knowledge to the Gunwinggu of Arnhem Land, Australia. But Lumaluma was greedy and whenever he saw people collecting anything tasty, such as sweet wild honey, he would declare the food *marelin*, or sacred, so that it was taboo to them, and he could eat it himself.

Wherever he went, Lumaluma taught the sacred rituals to the people. His wives scolded him because the people were starving, but he wouldn't listen; all he thought about was the the information he had to give. So the people trapped him on the beach and attacked him. Even as he lay dying he kept on teaching them the sacred rites. 'Spear me slowly,' he said, 'I still have more to teach you.' Lumaluma taught the rituals to the men, and his wives did the same for the women. When Lumaluma died, his body was left by the sea, and it slipped beneath the waves, transformed back into a whale.

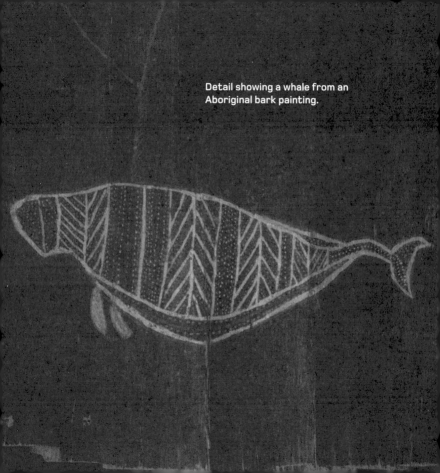

Detail showing a whale from an Aboriginal bark painting.

Uluru

Australia is not so much a landmass as a story mass to Aborigines. The land itself is a living myth; the myths give narrative life to the land. The sacred geography of Australia converges on Uluru, a large sandstone rock formation in the Northern Territory. It is perceived as the centre from which all the dreaming tracks in the Dreaming radiate. These are the 'songlines' that trace the travels of the ancestral beings. These dreaming tracks are thought of as the sinews, bones and internal organs of the living body of Australia, of which Uluru is the navel, not the heart. It is regarded by the Aborigines as a great storehouse of spiritual power, or *djang*.

Uluru was created during an epic battle between the Kunia, or carpet-snake people, and the Liru, the poisonous-snake people. Three rock holes high on Uluru mark the place where Ungata, the leader of the Kunia, bled to death. The water that spills from them is Ungata's blood. It flows down to fill the pool of the rainbow snake Wanambi.

The rainbow snake

The rainbow snake is an important figure in Aboriginal mythology. Rainbow snakes are both male and female, mammal and reptile. The snakes emerged from waterholes during the Dreaming. As they travelled the country, their movements created the hills, valleys and waterways of the ancestral landscape. Today a rainbow snake arches above the land as the rainbow, and can be seen in the scintillation of light on water, and in reflective substances such as quartz crystal and pearl shell.

Many myths tell of the dangers of irritating a rainbow snake or damaging its eggs; to do so causes the snake to send a flood, in which case a 'clever man' (a shaman) must dive into the floodwater to wrestle with the snake and make the flood recede. The healing powers of Aboriginal clever men are obtained from the rainbow snake. In northwestern Australia, shamanic candidates are swallowed by the snake, and reduced to the size of babies. These babies are taken to the sky world, killed, and brought back to life with quartz and little rainbow snakes in their bodies.

Eaglehawk and crow

Australian Aboriginal societies are divided into two moieties, or kinship groups, each with its own Dreaming ancestor. For the Kooris of modern Victoria, these two ancestors are Bunjil, the eaglehawk, and Bellin-Bellin, the crow. Bunjil is a very powerful creator who made the mountains and rivers, the flora and fauna, and also created humans and established the rules to be lived by.

After Bunjil had finished his creation, he asked Bellin-Bellin to open his dilly bag and let out the wind. When Bellin-Bellin opened the bag, such a ferocious wind swept out that it ripped the trees from the earth. Still Bunjil called for more, and Bellin-Bellin increased the force of the wind until Bunjil and his family, including his son Binbeal, the rainbow, were lifted up into the sky by a whirlwind. The Kooris believed that the sky was held up by four props. Soon after the first white men arrived, word passed that the eastern sky prop was rotting, causing consternation that soon proved all too justified.

Cave where Bunjil is said to have taken shelter in the Dreaming.

Myths of China

Chinese mythology is very diverse and complex. It spans some 5,000 years of civilization and features legends from more than 50 minority peoples, such as the Akha and Miao, as well as the majority Han Chinese. Classical Chinese myths were collected in texts such as *The Classic of Mountains and Seas* (third century BCE to second century CE).

From these early texts comes the story of the creation of the world by the giant Pan Gu, who is born from the cosmic egg of yin and yang. Other stories include that of Nu Gua, the creator of humanity, Yi, the heavenly archer, and Yu, the queller of the great flood. Yu was, for a long time, said to be the author of *The Classic of Mountains and Seas*. To these early, often fragmentary and hard-to-follow myths, has been added a vast pantheon of gods derived from the religions of Daoism, Confucianism, Buddhism and folk religion, all with their own stories. Gods were conceived as living in a heaven that mirrored the court of the Chinese emperor with, at its head, the supreme god, the Jade Emperor.

Guardian lions appear as mythical protectors in many Chinese folktales.

Pan Gu

In the beginning chaotic matter was contained inside an egg and the giant Pan Gu (Coiled Antiquity) was born in the middle of it. After 18,000 years, the egg opened. All the light 'yang' matter rose up to become the sky, and all the heavy 'yin' matter sank to form the earth. Between the sky and the earth, Pan Gu transformed himself nine times, becoming more divine than heaven and wiser than earth. Every day the heavens rose ten feet higher, and the earth grew ten feet thicker, and Pan Gu grew ten feet taller.

After another 18,000 years Pan Gu was fully grown, and the heavens and earth had also reached their full height. Pan Gu was exhausted by the effort of pushing heaven and earth apart. As he lay dying, he transformed himself one last time. His breath became the wind and clouds, his voice became the thunder. His left eye became the sun, his right eye became the moon, his hair and beard became the stars. All his bodily parts became elements of the physical world; even his sweat became the rain.

Nu Gua

When heaven and earth opened and the world came into being, human beings did not exist. The creator goddess Nu Gua (Woman Gua) had a human face but the body of a snake. She was lonely, so she took yellow clay and shaped it in her hands to make the first human beings. They came to life, and danced and sang. Nu Gua was pleased with her creations and kept making them, but she became tired before the world was anywhere near full. Nu Gua pulled a rope through mud. As she shook the mud off it, the splatters turned into more humans. Those made of yellow clay were the aristocrats; those made of mud were the common people, and there were many more of them.

Later myth gives Nu Gua a consort, her brother Fu Xi, and they were the first couple. When they entwined their tails to make love, they plaited grass to make a fan to hide their faces, which is why every Chinese bride holds a fan. Fu Xi invented writing, divination and hunting weapons; after observing a spider weaving its web, he taught humans how to make fishing nets.

The farmer god

The first people were hunter-gatherers. It was Shen Nong, the farmer god, who made the first plough and taught human beings how to sow all the different types of grain.

Shen Nong was also the god of medicine, whose discoveries laid down the rules of traditional Chinese herbal remedies, dividing every plant into four categories: bland, toxic, cool and hot. He thrashed each plant with his rust-coloured whip to release its essence, and personally smelled and tasted every single plant and every source of water to find out which were beneficial and which were poisonous. Doing this, he poisoned himself 70 times in a single day. Shen Nong's body was transparent, so he could see what effect each plant was having. One plant, the Bowel Breaking Weed, was so toxic that even Shen Nong could not withstand it and he died in the service of humanity.

Subsequently the gift of grain was attributed to another deity, Hou Ji (Sovereign Millet), who can be either female or male.

Yi and the ten suns

The sun goddess Xi He gave birth to ten suns in the form of three-legged ravens, which took it in turns to shine. Xi He drove them across the sky one at a time in her carriage drawn by six dragons. But in the time of Emperor Yao the suns grew bored of their routine and ran out into the sky all at once. Together, the ten suns were so hot they scorched the earth and burned the crops, and even the rocks began to melt.

Emperor Yao prayed to Di Jun, the Emperor of Heaven, who was the father of the suns, and Di Jun sent Yi, the heavenly archer, down to earth with his wife Chang-e. Yi tried to frighten the suns, but they were not intimidated, so Yi drew his bow and sent an arrow into the sky. The first sun exploded into fire and transformed into a raven as it fell to earth. Eight more arrows slew eight more suns.

Emperor Yao had to steal Yi's last arrow so that the world would still have warmth and light from the single remaining sun.

Yi shoots down the suns.

Chang-e

After the heavenly archer Yi slew nine of the ten suns and also rid the world of monsters, he and his wife Chang-e returned to heaven. Di Jun, the Emperor of Heaven, was not happy to see them because he was the father of the nine suns who had been killed. So he banished Yi and Chang-e to earth.

Chang-e did not like living on earth and was especially afraid of dying. So Yi went on a quest to the Queen Mother of the West, seeking the elixir of immortality. She gave him enough of the elixir for two people, warning him that the dose would be too much for one. Yi brought it home, to keep for an auspicious day, but Chang-e could not wait and drank it all herself. She felt her body becoming light and she floated upwards. She dared not return to heaven, so she went to the moon, where she lives out her immortality, transformed into a toad. She shares her loneliness with a hare and the alchemist Wu Kang. He, too, sought immortality and was exiled to the moon, condemned to eternally chop down an ever-renewing cassia tree (the tree of immortality).

Yu and the great flood

A great flood threatened to destroy the world. All the rivers broke their banks, and many people were drowned. The god Gun felt pity for the people and wanted to mend the riverbanks. With the aid of a divine owl, who knew all the mysteries of the sky, and a divine turtle, who knew all the secrets of the waters, Gun stole the miraculous breathing-earth – self-renewing soil that the god of heaven used for cosmic repair. But before he could finish his task, the god of heaven found out about the theft and sentenced him to death.

From Gun's body was born his son Yu (Reptilian Pawprint), who in some versions is envisaged as a man, but in others as a dragon. Yu was allowed to use the breathing-earth and, with its help, managed to repair the rivers. He created new waterways with the aid of the turtle, who carried the soil on its back, and the Responding Dragon, who divided the earth with its tail. Yu then slew a nine-headed monster that was polluting the soil with its drool. This enabled a new age of agriculture and human civilization.

Yu in the palace of Emperor Shun

The Jade Emperor

In the earliest Chinese myths, the supreme deity of the Shang people (c. 1600–1046 bce) is Shang Di. The Zhou people (1046–256 bce) called this god Tian Di. In the Song dynasty (960–1279 ce), this god acquired the name Yu Huang, the Jade Emperor. His court mirrors that of the emperor on earth, with a palace, servants, and a vast bureaucracy of lesser gods conceived almost as an army of civil servants, under the supervision of Yu Huang's chief minister Dongyue Dadi. Many of the immortal gods were once human and became immortal having achieved perfection, and they may come from Daoist, Confucian or Buddhist traditions. This is the case with Yu Huang. Originally a saintly human prince, he achieved perfection through an exceptional devotion to Daoism.

In one myth, after passing 3,200 trials, each lasting about three million years, the Jade Emperor discovers that an evil demon who had passed 3,000 trials has overcome the gods in heaven. Using his wisdom and benevolence, the Jade Emperor defeats the demon and is chosen by the grateful gods to be their leader.

The Eight Immortals

The word *xian*, immortal, literally means 'a man who lives on a mountain'. The Eight Immortals revered in Daoism are a group of eight figures who, though their backstories have little in common, are often depicted living and travelling together.

He Xian'gu is the only female. Sworn to virginity in her lifetime, she was the protectress of unmarried girls. Cao Guojiu left home in shame after his brother was executed for murder. Searching for the Dao, 'the Way', he met two other Immortals, the portly and flippant Zhongli Quan and his disciple, the philosopher Lü Dongbin. They asked him where the way was and he pointed to the sky. They asked him where the sky was and he pointed to his heart. Impressed, they taught him the secrets of perfection. The healing beggar Li Tieguai, the androgynous minstrel Lan Caihe, the hermit Zhang Guolao (who travels on a donkey he can fold up like a map) and the flautist Han Xiangzi complete the eight. For all their piety and wisdom, they are often depicted as enjoying life to the full.

Apoe Miyeh

The Akha hill tribe live in Yunnan province in southwest China. Over the last few centuries, they have also settled in the countries of the Golden Triangle – Thailand, Laos and Myanmar. They follow the Akhazan, 'the Akha way', a social and spiritual code that governs every aspect of life.

The village priest of an Akha village draws his sacred authority to deal with the spirit world from his direct link to the creator, Apoe Miyeh, whose name means 'male ancestor' in Akha. Apoe Miyeh created the earth and the sky. From the sky descended a series of spirits, the last of whom, Sm-mi-o, created human beings. These first humans knew nothing, but Apoe Miyeh handed out books to all the different peoples, containing all the knowledge they needed. The book Apoe Miyeh gave to the Akha was written on the skin of a water buffalo. There came a time when the Akha were so hungry they ate the buffalo skin, so now they carry the knowledge of Apoe Miyeh inside themselves, and have no need of books.

Akha man and woman

Weaving heaven and earth

The Miao live in the mountains of southern China, though some subgroups, such as the Hmong, have migrated into South East Asia. Their creation myth reflects the importance of weaving, sewing and embroidery in the lives of Miao women and girls.

When the sky was opened and the earth was dug up, the primal couple, Ntzï Tao Ntso Ntzï (god mountain fragment) and Ntzï Tao Ntso Bo (weave fragment woman), decided to weave the world. But they were already old, so they asked their daughters Tsu Ma Ngeo Dong and Ch'in Ntzï Dong Bu to do so. As they worked, they saw the people down below lying like rice husks on the earth, and the people up above lying like tree leaves in the sky, but nobody would help them. On the third day a girl named Ngeo Ge Ngeo Ntseo (willing young woman beautiful as a flower) came to help them. When they were finished they measured the earth and sky, and saw that the sky was wider than the earth. Ngeo Ge Ngeo Ntseo said, 'The sky is like a bamboo hat, the earth is like a winnowing basket.'

Miao batik baby-carrying quilt

Myths of Japan

Completed in 712 CE, *Kojiki*, the *Record of Ancient Things*, is the oldest book written in Japanese. It is at once a record of Japanese mythology and an account of the origins and history of the imperial clan. The sun goddess Amaterasu is regarded as the first ancestor of the imperial family. Her shrine at Ise, where she was worshipped in early times as the Great Heaven Shining Deity, was at first restricted to members of the imperial family.

Japanese mythology is also deeply entwined with the Shinto religion and its central notion of 'service to the *kami*'. The word *kami* can be translated either as 'gods' or 'sacred powers of nature'. There are an infinite number of *kami*. Some are great creative beings, some are natural forces, while others are the souls of ancestors. Another source of Japanese myths are the epic songs of the Ainu, the indigenous people of Japan. These tell stories of the gods and are sung in the first person, as if by the gods themselves.

Torii gate to a Shinto shrine

Izanami and Izanagi

Izanami and Izanagi were the first couple. They came down from heaven on the Rainbow Bridge and stirred the primal ocean with a spear to create Onogoro, the first island. Seeing a pair of wagtails mating, they felt desire. Walking around a pillar, they married, but because female Izanami spoke first, their first baby Hiruko was a leech-child, whom they set adrift on reeds.

They remarried, with Izanagi speaking first, and Izanami gave birth to the islands of Japan and to many *kami*, or gods. When she gave birth to the god of fire, Kagutsuchi, Izanami was so badly injured she died. Izanagi pursued her to Yomi, the underworld, begging her to return. He followed her down to plead with the gods of Yomi, breaking off a tooth from his comb to use as a torch. By this light he saw that her body was already rotting and full of maggots. Izanagi fled, pursued by Izanami and the hordes of Yomi. He just managed to seal the entrance with a rock, trapping her in death. For this, Izanami swore to kill 1,000 people a day, whereas Izanagi promised to create 1,500 new babies.

Susanoo

When Izanagi emerged from the underworld after failing to rescue his wife, he was filthy and polluted. Washing himself, he created more gods. The sun goddess Amaterasu came into being when he washed his right eye, the moon god Tsuki-Yomi when he washed his left eye, and the storm god Susanoo when he cleaned his nose.

Izanagi made Susanoo responsible for the sea, but Susanoo wept, and demanded instead to go to see his mother Izanami in Yomi, the underworld. Izanagi banished him from heaven. On his way, Susano defiled the sacred Weaving Hall of his sister Amaterasu. The gods punished him by cutting off his beard and nails, and sent him away to wander the world as an outcast. There he saved the Rice Paddy Princess from an eight-headed dragon, turning her into a comb that he stuck in his hair. He got the dragon drunk on sake and killed it. In the dragon's tail was the sword Kusanagi, which Susanoo gave to Amaterasu in apology. Then he turned the Rice Paddy Princess back into a girl and married her.

Amaterasu

The sun goddess Amaterasu and her maidens wove the fabric of the universe in her sacred Weaving Hall. When her brother, the storm god Susanoo, broke down her rice paddies, defecated in the Hall of the First Fruits and dropped a flayed pony through the roof of the Weaving Hall, Amaterasu was so shocked she fled and hid in a cave, closing its entrance with a stone. Both heaven and earth went dark.

Without sun, nothing would grow. The gods tried everything to tempt Amaterasu out, to no avail. At last Omoshi-kane, the thought-combining god, asked the goddess of dawn Ama-no-uzume to perform a striptease on an upturned sake tub. The gods laughed so hard at her antics, it drew Amaterasu to the mouth of the cave, asking what the fuss was about. Ama-no-uzume told her they were celebrating the arrival of a goddess who shone more brightly than Amaterasu. When she came out to see, they dazzled her with her own reflection in a mirror and pulled her out of the cave, sealing it with a sacred rope so she could never return.

Amaterasu emerges
from her cave.

The origin of rice

When the sun goddess Amaterasu heard that the goddess of food Ogetsu was in the Central Land of the Reed Plains, she sent her brother Tsuki-Yomi, the moon god, to see what she was doing. By the time Tsuki-Yomi found Ogetsu he was hungry and rudely demanded to be fed. Affronted, Ogetsu began vomiting and excreting a feast for him. Tsuki-Yomi, in turn, was so annoyed to be offered such polluted food that he drew his sword and slew Ogetsu. From her body grew all the staple crops of Japan. Rice sprang from her eyes, millet from her ears, wheat from her genitals and soybeans from her rectum. Cows and horses emerged from her forehead, and silkworms from her eyebrows.

When Tsuki-Yomi revealed what he had done to Amaterasu, she disowned him, which is why the sun and moon are rarely seen together in the sky. Then Amaterasu sent for all the things that had grown from Ogetsu's body, so she could distribute them to mankind.

Inari, god of rice

Inari is the god of rice, the staple crop of Japan. He may appear as a bearded man, as a woman or as a fox. Although generally mistrusted in Japan, foxes are regarded as messengers of Inari.

One story tells of a farmer who married a woman who was Inari in human form. He was happy with her until, one night, he saw a fox's brush hanging below the edge of the quilt. In another version, he found her brushing the yard with her tail. Either way, the farmer realized he had married a fox. Nevertheless he stayed with her, and she even helped him to cheat the taxman by showing him how to sow his rice upside down, meaning that the crop was hidden beneath the water.

Inari comes down from his home in the mountains every spring, along with the mountain streams that replenish the paddy fields, and returns every autumn. Because rice is a symbol of wealth, Inari is also the god of merchants.

The deity of rice, Inari, can be depicted as a woman, a man or a fox — or sometimes accompanied by a fox.

Benten

Benten is the only female member of the Shichi Fukujin, the seven gods of good fortune. Besides Benten (or Benzaiten), the goddess of love and the arts, they are Bishamon, the god of protection; Daikoku, the god of prosperity; Ebisu, the god of luck; Fukurokuju, the god of wisdom; Hotei, the god of generosity; and Jurojin, the god of longevity. These seven gods are often depicted together in their wonderful treasure ship.

Benten is the goddess of music, and always carries a stringed instrument called a *biwa*. She will appear to musicians who play with all their soul. She is also the goddess of everything that flows, including the sea and the river that flows from Mount Meru. Once she appealed to a serpent king who was terrorizing the countryside. Though she was initially repulsed, the serpent wooed her with such silken words that, when he agreed to refrain from his savagery, she agreed to marry him. People in need of money often pray to Benten for, as the serpent proved, she can be won over by eloquent words.

Mount Fuji

The word *kami* can mean either 'gods' or 'sacred powers of nature'. All living things and natural features have a *kami*. Mount Fuji is believed to embody a powerful female *kami* known as Kaguya-hime. This *kami* must always be approached with reverence, as the followers of the 12th-century hero Tadatsune found to their cost when they trespassed on her territory. She appeared on the far side of an underground river with a dragon by her side, and those who crossed were instantly killed.

Long ago an old man found a baby girl on the mountain and called her Kaguya-hime. She grew up to be so beautiful that the Japanese emperor married her. Seven years later she declared that she was immortal, and must return to heaven. To console him, she gave him a mirror in which he would always be able to see her. Using the mirror, he followed Kaguya-hime all the way to the top of Mount Fuji. Once there, however, he found he could follow no further. His thwarted passion set the mirror ablaze, which is why smoke is always seen rising from the mountaintop.

Kamuy creates the land and the people

Kotan-kor-kamuy (land-making deity) is the Ainu creator. In the beginning, the earth was a lifeless swamp, with six heavens above and six worlds below.

One day Kotan-kor-kamuy sent a wagtail down to the swamp to make land. The poor bird had no idea how to do this. In a panic, it started to beat the water with its tail and slowly the land began to emerge. The new world was so beautiful that the animals that lived with Kotan-kor-kamuy in the heavens begged him to let them live there. He agreed.

Then Kotan-kor-kamuy created the Ainu people, with earth bodies, chickweed hair and willow-stick spines that bend with age. Then he sent Aeoina-kamuy (the god about whom we sing) to teach the people rituals and crafts, and how to hunt and cook. Aeoina-kamuy is also known as Ainurakkur (he with a human-Ainu smell), because when he returned to heaven the other gods complained that he stank of human beings.

Ainu hunters

The fire goddess

Also known as Grandmother Hearth, Fuchi, the goddess of fire, is important to Ainu ritual. She protects the house and its occupants. When a fire is ritually sprinkled with sake, Fuchi carries prayers to the *kamuy* – god-like spirits who pervade all parts of the world.

The hearth, the miniature universe in which Fuchi lives, is at the centre of a traditional Ainu house. At the east end of the room is a small sacred window that provides both an entrance and an exit for gods such as Kimun-kamuy, the bear god. He is central to the *iyomante* ceremony in which the Ainu thank him for there always being enough bears to sustain them. The ceremony starts with a prayer to Fuchi, who mediates between the Ainu and the *kamuy*.

One myth tells how Fuchi engaged in a magic contest with the goddess of water Wakka-ush-Kamuy, who had stolen away Fuchi's husband. Fuchi wins, and her husband returns, sheepish and cowed, to sit meekly at her hearth.

Hearth at the centre
of a traditional
Japanese house

Myths of India

Much of the subtle and complex mythology of India is incorporated in the Hindu religion, but has roots in the Indus civilization (c. 2500–1500 BCE), where it seems the god of creation and destruction Siva and the great goddess Devi were already worshipped. This early mythology then merged with the Vedic gods of the Aryans, who invaded India c. 1700 BCE. This blended mythology was first written down in the Rig-Veda c. 1200 BCE.

Many of the important Vedic gods, such as the sky god Indra, the sun god Surya, Agni, the god of fire and sacrifice, and Yama, the god of death, are still worshipped. Often, they take a reduced role in the vast pantheon of Hindu gods and goddesses, all of whom are aspects of Brahman, the essential creative power of the universe. Besides the great Hindu gods Brahma, Siva and Vishnu, Indian mythology also includes rich tribal mythologies, particularly well recorded in Central India and the Northeast Frontier, preserving the stories and beliefs of the Baiga and Singpho peoples, among others.

Brahma, the creator

The earliest Hindu mythology tells of a supreme god called Prajapati, who produced all living things through acts of incest with his daughter, in different animal forms. This god has been assimilated into Brahma, the creator.

Brahma has four heads – he used to have five, but Siva cut one off when Brahma claimed to be his superior. Brahma is the lord of space-time. Every *kalpa*, which lasts 4,320 million human years, Brahma recreates the world; each *kalpa* is but a day and a night to him. In the night of Brahma, when chaos rules, the god Vishnu sleeps on the snake Ananta in the cosmic ocean. At dawn a lotus grows from Vishnu's navel, containing Brahma, ready to make the world anew. At first Brahma is still drowsy and makes mistakes; hence, the world is never perfect. Only through meditation can Brahma see both the beginning and the end of the universe and fully utilize his creative powers. The world we experience is simply an ever-changing illusion breathed out by Brahma, called *maya*.

The churning
of the ocean

The myth of the churning of the ocean is found in the Hindu epic, the *Mahabharata*. The gods gathered on Mount Meru to discuss how to obtain the *amrita*, or elixir of immortality, which was hidden in the depths of the ocean. Vishnu suggested they churn it out, using the serpent Vasuki, king of the Nagas, as the twisting rope, and Mount Meru itself as the paddle. The Devas (gods) grasped the serpent by one end and the Asuras (demons), who had been promised a share of the elixir, pulled from the other. Soon the ocean turned into butter and from it emerged fourteen precious things, including the sun, the moon, Vishnu's wife Lakshmi, Surabhi, the cow of plenty, and finally Dhanvantari, the physician of the gods, bearing the precious elixir.

Vishnu did not want the Asuras to taste the elixir and achieve immortality, so he tricked them by turning into a beautiful girl. Only one Asura, Rahu the grasper, won a sip; Vishnu cut off his head. This head is immortal, and constantly swallows and regurgitates the moon, ravenous for another taste of the precious *amrita*.

The avatars of Vishnu

Vishnu, the protector and restorer of the world, has come to earth in human or animal form nine times so far, according to one version of the story. When he comes a tenth time, as Kalkin, the white horse, the end of this era will have arrived.

Vishnu's first avatar was Matsya, the fish, who warned Manu, the first man, of a coming deluge and told him to build an ark. As the tortoise Kurma, he provided a base for Mount Meru at the churning of the ocean. As the wild boar Varaha, he saved the world from the demon Hiranyaksha. As the man-lion Narasimha and as the dwarf Vamana, he defeated demon kings. Vamana begged the demon king Bali for as much land as he could cover in three strides – and in three strides he covered the whole world, leaving Bali only the underworld. As the axeman Parashurama, he asserted the supremacy of the scholarly Brahman caste over the warrior caste. As Rama, he slew the demon Ravana. As Krishna, he wooed Radha and defeated demons. Finally, as the Buddha, he taught humankind the path to enlightenment.

The list of Vishnu's avatars varies across India and often incorporates regional deities that increase the number.

Siva and Parvati

Siva (or Shiva), the destroyer, was so distressed at the suicide of his wife Sati that he began dancing the ferocious Tandava dance that would bring about the end of the world before its time. The gods were so alarmed that Vishnu reincarnated Sati as the gentle, beautiful Parvati, daughter of Mount Himalaya.

When Parvati playfully covered Siva's eyes with her hands, the world went dark, and Siva instantly grew a third eye on his foreheard, which blazes with the fire of ten million suns. When Kama, the god of love, interrupted Siva's meditation with thoughts of desire for Parvati, Siva inadvertently opened his third eye and reduced Kama to ash, so the god of love is now *ananga*, bodiless.

When Siva and Parvati made love, the whole world trembled, for though Siva is the god of ascetics, he is also the god of the sacred phallus. He is worshipped as the lord of the dance, in which he dances the creation and destruction of the world, and is often depicted dancing in a circle of flames.

Skanda and Ganesha

Skanda, the god of war, and Ganesha, the remover of obstacles and god of wisdom and learning, were the two children of Siva and Parvati. Despite Siva being an expert at love, and Parvati desiring nothing more than his embrace, the conception of both children was highly unusual.

The other gods disturbed the couple's lovemaking, hoping Siva would aid them against the demon Taraka, who was eventually killed by Skanda. Siva's spilled seed journeyed on a convoluted route in the river Ganges, before being born as six boys. Parvati cuddled them so tight that they merged into a single body with six heads – Skanda.

Parvati, rendered barren by the intervention of the gods, made Ganesha from the scrapings of her body after she bathed. Later, when Ganesha tried to prevent Siva from disturbing Parvati's bath, Siva burned his head off, so it was replaced with the head of an elephant.

Ganesha, the elephant-headed god

Durga and the demons

The Great Goddess Devi contains all the goddesses within herself. Many of these are benevolent – Lakshmi the goddess of good fortune, Sarasvati, the wise wife of Brahma, Parvati, the gentle wife of Siva. Other forms are frightening and violent, such as Kali, the four-armed goddess of death, with her necklace of skulls.

As a warrior, Devi was incarnated as Durga, 'the unapproachable', created by the collective anger of the gods when they were evicted from Mount Meru by the buffalo demon Mahisha and his army of Asuras (demons). Durga rode into battle on a lion, slaying every demon in her path. Mahisha responded by shattering the earth with his hooves, tossing mountains into the air with his horns and overflowing the oceans with the lashing of his tail. At last Durga faced the buffalo demon in single combat. With her foot on his neck, Durga forced the spirit from Mahisha's mouth, and cut off his head. As he died, all the creatures in the world cried, 'Victory!' The demon hordes wailed as they were destroyed, and all the gods rejoiced.

Durga, the
unapproachable
warrior goddess

Rama and Sita

The epic Hindu poem *Ramayana* tells the story of Rama, the seventh avatar of Vishnu, sent by Brahma to vanquish the demon king Ravana. Rama and his three brothers were born to a childless king, and each shared some of Vishnu's divinity.

Ravana abucted Rama's wife Sita – born from the earth as her father ploughed a furrow – and took her to the island of Lanka. Rama sought the help of Sugriva, the monkey king, who lent him his general Hanuman. At the siege of Lanka, Hanuman led a monkey army against Ravana's army of demons. Rama borrowed the chariot and charioteer of the sky god Indra to pursue Ravana himself, but every time he cut off one of Ravana's ten heads, another grew in its place. Finally Rama killed Ravana with an arrow forged by Brahma. At first Rama rejected the rescued Sita, but after the gods testified to her purity, they lived happily for 10,000 years. Told his subjects still thought her impure, Rama then sent Sita into exile. Years later he asked her to return, but her heart was broken, and she sank back into the earth.

Rama and Sita seek counsel from the sage Bharadvaja.

Agni, the god of fire and sacrifice

Agni, the god of fire and sacrifice, is reborn wherever a fire is lit. He has two heads, a body as red as fire and seven tongues to lick up the butter offered in his sacrifices to the gods.

Agni consumes and purifies the dirt and sin of the world. This purifying power was granted to him by the sage Bhrigu, after Agni had told a wronged husband that his wife was in Bhrigu's house. Bhrigu first cursed Agni to eat everything in his path, but when Agni argued that as a god he had to tell the truth, Bhrigu gave him the power to purify everything he burnt.

Agni was one of the chief Vedic gods of early India, along with Indra and Surya, but his role was gradually usurped by both Siva, the destroyer, and Skanda, the god of war. During the course of Skanda's complicated gestation and birth, Agni is briefly and agonizingly pregnant with the god, having gobbled up the burning seed of Siva in the form of a dove. Earlier myths, equally complex, have Agni as Skanda's father.

The Singpho creation

The creation myths of the Singpho reflect their environment in the foothills of the Himalayas. In the beginning there was no earth or sky, just cloud and mist. From this was born a cloud-woman named Khupning-Knam. In time she gave birth to a snow-girl called Ningon-Chinun and a snow-boy, Tum-Kam-Waisun.

When they grew up Ningon-Chinun and Tum-Kam-Waisun married, and from them were born a mud-girl called Inga (Earth) and a cloud-boy called Mu (Sky). They had a son called Imbung (Wind). When he was born his first breath was so strong that it blew his father up into the sky, and dried up his mother, and so heaven and earth were made. The supreme being Phan-Ninsang explored this new world with the sky god Mathum-Matta. They found a gourd in the shape of a man, and when they broke it open a host of little people poured out. These were the first human beings, and they lived up with the gods on a heavenly plateau, until there were too many of them, at which point they came down to earth on ladders of bamboo and wood.

Himalayan foothills

Nanga Baiga

The Baiga of the Mandla hills in central India believe that they have lived as guardians of the forest since the dawn of time. They are the sons and daughters of Dharti Mata, Mother Earth. The Baiga hero, Nanga Baiga, was the very first man on earth. He was born in the forest from Mother Earth herself, and nursed beneath a clump of bamboos by Bamboo Girl. Nanga Baigin, the first woman, was born alongside him.

Bhagavan, the creator, had spread the world out flat like a chapati, but it flapped about and would not stay still. Nanga Baiga and Nanga Baigin took four great nails and drove them into the four corners of the earth to steady it. Bhagavan said, 'Kings may lose their kingdoms, but you will never lose the jungle. You are made of the earth and are lord of the earth, and shall never forsake it. You must guard the earth, and keep its nails in place.' He told Nanga Baiga he would always be poor, but that was good, for only the poor would be content to be the servants of Dharti Mata.

Baiga women

Creation myths

Myths of the creation of the cosmos, the earth and sky, of human beings and animals, occur in virtually all cultures, often with multiple and contradictory variants. At times the first beings are almost abstract forces, like the deities Vacant and Empty in the Native-American Juaneño creation myth, or Babylonian Apsu and Tiamat, the sweet water and the salt. The creator may emerge from a primal ocean, like the ancient Egyptian Ra, from a chasm as in ancient Greek and Norse myth, or from an egg, as in the Polynesian myth of Tangaroa's creation. Tangaroa is an example of the world being made from the body parts of a creator or a primal being, a pattern repeated with Chinese Pan Gu, Norse Ymir and Aztec Tlaltecuhtli.

The need to explain the origin of the world is deeply rooted in humanity. Only one human culture has been discovered without creation myths, the Pirahãs of the Amazon. Asked what came first, the Pirahãs told no sacred stories about cosmic eggs or primal oceans. Pressed, the best they could come up with was 'bananas'.

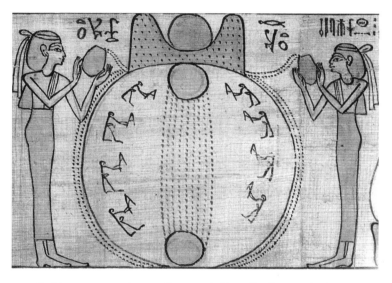

Goddesses pour waters on the mound of creation in an ancient
Egyptian manuscript.

Flood myths

Myths of a great flood that devastates the earth are found in many cultures, the earliest being in Mesopotamia, where the 'Noah figure' builds an ark and survives. Very similar stories are found in India and ancient Greece among other cultures. On the plains of North America, the Mandan believed that the world had been destroyed by flood once before, when the only survivor was Lone Man, and that humanity would be overwhelmed by flood again if they did not dance their sacred Buffalo Dance. Even continental Europe has its own flood myth, in the Slovenian story of Kranyatz, the sole survivor of the flood who then vied with the Dionysos-like trickster Kurent for rulership of the earth, only to be undone by his love of wine. There are also widespread myths in which the world is devastated not by flood, but by a great fire.

Nobody can explain this commonality. Rather than preserving memories of actual disasters, it is most likely that these myths symbolize human resilience, showing that, even after almost total destruction, humankind can pick itself up and start again.

The Hindu hero Manu rescues his family from a world-destroying deluge

Heroes and heroines

Mythological heroes are often semi-divine, like Gilgamesh, Herakles or Cuchulain. They are heroes, not because all their actions are admirable, but because they are larger than life, distinguished by their great strength, courage or ingenuity, as in the case of the cunning Odysseus.

Unlike goddesses, who tend to be strong figures who compete with gods on equal terms, the heroines of mythology tend to be great beauties or doomed lovers – for example, Helen of Troy or Deirdre of the Sorrows. A feisty spirit like Arachne, who arrogantly competes with the goddess Athena and makes fun of the gods, is rare and she is punished for her presumption.

A special kind of hero who teaches people their crafts and laws is called a culture hero – for example, Aeoina-kamuy of the Japanese Ainu or a tribal ancestor such as Nanga Baiga, or the Real People of an even earlier mythical race – the *woge* – who instituted the laws and customs of the California Yurok tribe.

Ajax carrying the body of Achilles, depicted on a Greek urn of *c.* 500 BCE

Quests

A quest is a special sort of adventure, made in search of either a tangible or intangible treasure. In Greek mythology the Quest of the Golden Fleece enacts a pattern still familiar today. In order to achieve his prize, Jason gathers a crew of Greek heroes including Herakles and Orpheus to join him for one last adventure.

Jason's quest is fulfilled, but not all such journeys end in triumph. The Mesopotamian hero Gilgamesh sets out in search of the secret of immortality, but loses it when he finds it. Even the most famous mission of all, the quest of the Holy Grail, yields a bittersweet victory. While Sir Galahad, pure in heart and mind, achieves the Grail, his success sets in motion the dissolution of the Round Table and the death of King Arthur. Quests are not always for treasure or victory – the quest of the ancient Greek Aeneas is to found a new nation after the fall of Troy, while that of Native-American Hiawatha is for peace and harmony.

Detail from *The Achievement of the Grail* tapestry by Edward Burne Jones and William Morris.

Tricksters

Trickster figures often provide a comic element and form a bridge between humanity and the gods. Native-American myth is alive with tricksters, such as Coyote, Raven and Hare, each of whom may play the role of culture hero or co-creator and is celebrated for getting into and out of scrapes.

In Africa, the tricksters are usually Hare and Spider – Anansi, the trickster hero of the Asante, for example. The Oceanic hero Maui is known as 'Maui-of-a-thousand-tricks'; even his death is an occasion of laughter. The Mayan Hero Twins Hunahpu and Xbalanque exhibit trickster characteristics when they deceive the death gods into allowing themselves to be killed.

The Greek hero Odysseus is most celebrated for his cunning and trickery in devising the Trojan Horse that enables the Greeks to overthrow Troy. Loki provides the dynamic for many of the Norse myths – his final, devastating trick bringing about the death of Balder the Beautiful.

Odysseus tricks the cyclops Polyphemus.

Death

Many mythologies have accounts as to how death came into the world. Sometimes it happens almost by accident – for example, when the San hare angers the moon. At other times it is deliberate, as in the Caduveo story of Caracara who comes bitterly to regret it.

An underworld land of the dead is another common feature, with vengeful deities such as Hine-nui-te-po in Polynesia or stern but fair gods like the ancient Greek Hades. For some mythologies, notably in Mesoamerica and ancient Egypt, the afterlife was a central theme; the desire to secure new life after death was the great focus of Egyptian ritual and belief.

Some heroes, such as Gilgamesh, sought immortality, while others ventured into the land of death, like Orpheus and King Arthur. For the Vikings, those who died in battle or sacrifice went to Odin, those who drowned went to the sea goddess Ran, and those who died of illness or old age went down to the gloom of Hel.

Orpheus mourns the
death of Eurydice.

The end of the world

Just as mythologies tell of the creation of the cosmos, so too they often foretell the end of all things. Some myths envisage the end to be final, but many more imply cycles of creation, destruction and new creation. Ragnarok, the twilight of the Norse gods, was foretold from the start. Although the ancient Egyptians spoke of 'millions and millions of years', they knew that the day would come when the sun god Ra would destroy all he had created, returning to the primal ocean to await a new cycle of creation.

For some, this imperfect world will be replaced at the end by a perfect one. In Zoroastrian belief, with the coming of the saviour Saoshyant, people will become pure and no longer in need of sustenance. Ahura Mazda, the Good Mind, will cast his evil brother Ahriman out of creation, and time will come to an end. Saoshyant will raise the dead, and each man and woman will pass through a stream of molten metal, and emerge purified. The new world will last for ever, free of the taint of evil.

Kalki is the final avatar of Vishnu, foretold to appear at the end of the world in Hindu scripture.

Key source texts

Aeneid
Between 29 and 19 BCE
An important Latin text, the *Aeneid* is
an epic poem by the best-known poet
of the Roman Empire, Virgil. It relates
the story of the Trojan hero Aeneas.

Book of the Dead
c. 1250 BCE
The ancient Egyptian *Book of the
Dead*, more accurately, *The Spells for
Coming Forth by Day*, is a collection of
spells to secure new life after death,
originating from the early Pyramid
and Coffin texts.

Enuma Elish
18th–16th centuries BCE
The *Enuma Elish* is the creation myth
of ancient Babylon, ritually recited
at the Akitu festival, the Babylonian
New Year.

Epic of Gilgamesh
c. 19th century BCE
This epic poem from ancient
Mesopotamia tells the story of
Gilgamesh, King of Uruk. It is thought
to be the earliest surviving great
work of literature.

Fasti
c. 8 CE
An unfinished work by the Roman
poet Ovid, centred on the Roman
religious calendar.

Historia des Nuevo Mundo
1653
Written by Father Bernabe Cobo to
record 'the false religion that the
Indians of Peru had', the *Historia des
Nuevo Mundo* is now better known as
Inca Religion and Customs.

Historia General de las Cosas de Nueva España
16th century
The General History of Things of New Spain by Bernadino de Sahagún recorded the myths of the Aztecs.

Iliad
c. 7th century BCE
A work of ancient Greek literature by Homer, the *Iliad* is an epic poem that centres on the Trojan War.

Kalevala
1849
The Finnish national mythological epic was compiled from folk poetry by Elias Lönnrot.

Kojiki, The Record of Ancient Things
712 CE
Kojiki, The Record of Ancient Things, recounts the mythological origins of the four main Japanese islands. It is an important early record of Shinto myths and imperial history.

Kumulipo
19th century
The Hawaiian creation chant *Kumulipo*, which translates as 'beginning-in-deep-darkness', first printed in 1889, was sacred to the ruling chiefs. It established the divine origin of their rule and traced its history to the beginning of the world.

Library of Mythology
c. 1st or 2nd century CE
Attributed to the ancient Greek scholar, Apollodorus, this compendium of Greek myths and heroic legends is arranged in three volumes.

The Mabinogion
12th–13th century
Originating in Wales, and based on centuries of oral tradition, *The Mabinogion* is considered the earliest example of prose legend and myth in British literature.

Metamorphoses
c. 8th century CE
A collection of some 250 stories sharing the common theme of transformation, written in the style of epic poetry by the Roman poet, Ovid.

Morte d'Arthur
15th century
First published in 1485 by William Caxton, *Le Morte d'Arthur* is, perhaps, the best known of several works of Arthurian literature in the English language. The Arthurian legends began in Wales, and spread down through Brittany right across Europe. Thomas Malory's *Morte d'Arthur* is essentially an English translation of French texts about King Arthur and the Knights of the Round Table.

Odyssey
c. 7th century BCE
The *Odyssey* is an epic poem written by the ancient Greek, Homer. It focuses on Odysseus's journey home following the Trojan War.

Popol Vuh

c. 1550

Popol Vuh, the *Book of Counsel*, records the history of the Quiché Maya people of Guatemala, and is the chief source of Mayan mythology.

Prose Edda

13th century

This Norse work was written by Snorri Sturluson to record and explain myths in the earlier *Poetic Edda*; in some cases, Snorri's versions of are the only ones that remain.

Rig Veda

1200 BCE

The Indian *Rig Veda* is the first record of Indian myths, supplemented by other Vedic writings, the epics *Mahabharata* and *Ramayana*, and the Puranas.

Shan Hai Jing

3rd century BCE

The *Shan Hai Jing* or *Classic of Mountains and Seas* is a mythic geography of China before the first Imperial dynasty, and major source of early Chinese mythology.

The Táin

12th century

Also known as *The Cattle Raid of Cooley*, *The Táin* is an epic work of early Irish literature, recounting the war between Ulster and Connaught, and the exploits of the hero, Cuchulain.

Theogony

c. 700 BCE

An epic poem written by the ancient Greek, Hesiod, *Theogony* relates the myths of the Greek gods.

Index

Quercus

New York · London

Text © 2017 by Neil Philip
First published in the United States by
Quercus in 2017

ISBN 978-1-68144-062-0

Library of Congress Control Number:
2017942570

Distributed in the United States and Canada
by Hachette Book Group
1290 Avenue of the Americas
New York, NY 10104

Manufactured in China

10 9 8 7 6 5 4 3 2 1

www.quercus.com

Picture credits 2: Shutterstock/David OBrien ; 9: Shutterstock/
Zwiebackesser; 13: Zouavman Le Zouave via Wikimedia; 15: C messier via
Wikipedia; 17: Dbachmann via Wikimedia; 37: Osama Shukir Muhammed
Amin FRCP via Wikimedia; 41: Anna Carotti via Wikimedia; 45: Jebulon
via Wikimedia; 47: Chipdawes via Wikimedia; 53: Deutsche Fotothek via
Wikimedia; 63: BabelStone via Wikimedia; 65: Mike Peel via Wikimedia; 67:
Urban via Wikimedia; 71: Maur via Wikimedia; 73: Mbzt via Wikimedia; 77:
Sailko via Wikimedia; 85: Shutterstock/BlackMac; 99: Marie-Lan Nguyen
via Wikimedia; 120: Sailko via Wikimedia; 133: Paul via Wikimedia; 149:
Camelia.boban via Wikimedia; 151: Mbdortmund via Wikimedia; 159: Jean-
Pol Grandmont via Wikimedia; 161: Rosemania via Wikimedia; 163: Siren-
Com via Wikimedia; 209: Geni via Wikimedia; 217: FA2010 via Wikimedia;
219: Shutterstock/Rozilynn Mitchell; 221: Shutterstock/LeshaBu; 225:
Shutterstock/Daria Rosen; 227: Shutterstock/ GeorgeColePhoto; 229:
She-we-na via Wikimedia; 235: Shutterstock/Mykola Mazuryk; 245:
John Sylvester/Alamy Stock Photo ; 247: Shutterstock/LeshaBu; 257:
Shutterstock/Carlos Romero; 261: James via Wikimedia; 267: Jkolecki
via Wikimedia; 275: Shutterstock/Christian Vinces; 277: Shutterstock/
Jess Kraft; 283: Shutterstock/Ingehogenbijl; 287: Brooklyn Museum
via Wikimedia; 291: Eric Lafforgue/Alamy Stock Photo; 293: Brooklyn
Museum via Wikimedia; 295: Shutterstock/Boyusya; 297: Shutterstock/
Wcpmedia; 299: Ivy Close Images/Alamy Stock Photo ; 301: Shutterstock/
Stefan Holm; 307: Shutterstock/Greg Ward NZ; 309: Avenue via
Wikimedia; 311: Shutterstock/Neftali; 313: Shutterstock/Mmtsales; 315:
Shutterstock/ChameleonsEye; 319: Shutterstock/ Mai Phongsook; 321:
Shutterstock/SherSS; 323: Heritage Image Partnership Ltd/Alamy Stock;
325: Shutterstock/FiledIMAGE; 327: Shutterstock/Craig Sutton; 329:
Michael Barnett via Wikimedia; 331: Shutterstock/Tratong; 351: Daderot
via Wikimedia; 361: Mary Evans/Grenville Collins Postcard Collection;
365: 663highland via Wikimedia; 371: Shutterstock/Hachi888; 373:
Shutterstock/Saiko3p ; 375: Jean-Pierre Dalbéra via Wikimedia; 379: Steve
Jurvetson via Wikimedia; 385: Shutterstock/Liudmila Kotvitckaia; 393:
Ekta Parishad via Wikimedia; 399: Bibi Saint-Pol via Wikimedia; 407: Art
Collection 3/Alamy Stock Photo.
All other illustrations by Tim Brown